CULT FILMMAKERS

CULT FILMMAKERS

50 movie mavericks you need to know

IAN HAYDN SMITH

WHITE LION
PUBLISHING

CONTENTS

INTRODUCTION

What makes a cult film, or characterises its filmmaker as a cult figure? Has the perception of what makes a cult film altered over the course of the medium's history? And is there a link between the early magical worlds of Georges Méliès, the taboo-breaking dramas of Tod Browning and the more recent, ultra-violent work of S. Craig Zahler (*Dragged Across Concrete*, 2018) or Panos Cosmatos (*Mandy*, 2018), directors whose films have crossed over from niche into the mainstream?

That none of the above names are among the 50 featured in this book is some indication of the breadth of filmmakers for whom the label 'cult' has been applied to their work. But these directors are good examples of where to start when understanding what a cult film is and the components that define it.

A cult film can be seen as something that lacks the appeal of more mainstream fare, bringing to audiences an extra factor that can range from the challenging to the kitsch. A film can acquire cult status immediately or after the passing of time and a gradual enhancing of its reputation. It may take more than a generation to fully acknowledge a film's cult appeal, with a shift in cultural tastes conferring on it a sense of importance or popularity that it never had when it was first screened. It can be regarded as ahead of its time, misunderstood by original audiences, or, in the case of a film whose quality is dubious, enjoyed for all the reasons that an audience disliked it in the first place. Edward D. Wood Jr. is arguably the best example of the kind of filmmaker whose movies, most famously *Plan 9 from Outer Space* (1959), are so bad they are good. His legacy lies in the hands of filmmakers such as Tommy Wiseau, whose *The Room* (2003) is widely acknowledged as one of the worst films ever made. But

Wiseau is now a cult figure, who not only travels the world to attend screenings of his film, but also was the subject of a Golden Globe-winning 'making of' feature, *The Disaster Artist* (2017).

Browning is no less a cult filmmaker than Wood or Wiseau, but his status was achieved through the shock of the unusual. *Freaks* (1932), a film about a troupe of sideshow performers, was notorious upon first release – and was banned in many countries – but its reputation and number of admirers have only grown with time. Browning ranks alongside Benjamin Christensen as one of the key cult filmmakers in cinema's first 50 years. (Christensen was chosen over Browning for inclusion in this collection solely for the utter strangeness of his 1922 hybrid documentary *Häxan*.) But is either more of a cult filmmaker than James Whale? Another director who was working when sound became an integral part of cinema and was primarily associated with horror, Whale differs only in that *Frankenstein* (1931) and *Bride of Frankenstein* (1935) were more commercially appealing productions that achieved significant box-office success. However, as a personality, he has become more of a cult figure.

The line between commercially popular and cult films is also blurred in film noir, the thriller subgenre that developed throughout the 1940s and 1950s. Billy Wilder's *Double Indemnity* (1944) and Howard Hawks' *The Big Sleep* (1946) are stylised and morally ambivalent films, but it is Edgar G. Ulmer's *Detour* (1945) and Robert Aldrich's *Kiss Me Deadly* (1955) that have gained cult status. In the case of Ulmer, his is a low-budget sliver of a feature (its drama is played out in a crisp 68 minutes) that was initially overlooked and so became a 'discovered' pleasure. Aldrich's near-

hallucinatory movie is the more obvious cult contender: a drama that pushes at the boundaries of the genre and ends with a nuclear apocalypse.

The popularity of cult films increased significantly from the late 1960s. In the United States, the failure of the studio system to reflect changes in audience tastes resulted in a search beyond the mainstream for films that entertained or challenged. A similar sentiment existed in other countries, where social mores were in a state of flux and traditional films evinced a moral, political or cultural perspective that spoke only to more conservative tastes. Film movements exploded these ideas, offering a vibrant alternative to the status quo and frequently challenging film form.

One side effect of this revolution was the midnight movie: a film whose appeal lay beyond the mainstream and whose popularity was first tested on audiences happy to watch films late into the night. The Elgin Theater in New York became the spiritual home of the midnight movie, a mecca for this new kind of film. And at the vanguard of this wave was Alejandro Jodorowsky's trippy western of sorts, *El Topo* (1970), in which the director plays a vengeful gunslinger, venting his wrath on ideologies that form the bastion of the world's civilisations. It was less a film to enjoy than an experience in which to immerse oneself, with the consumption of illicit substances a likely boon in furthering the enjoyment of time spent in Jodorowsky's strange universe. That film was joined by John Waters' early work, *The Harder They Come* (1972), Jim Sharman's *The Rocky Horror Picture Show* (1975) and David Lynch's beautiful and strange fever dream *Eraserhead* (1977). At the same time, in Italy, horror filmmakers were pushing the

boundaries of art and taste, first with Giallo – a subgenre of horror – and then beyond, reaching new heights of grotesque and unpleasantness with Ruggero Deodato's *Cannibal Holocaust* (1980) and Lucio Fulci's *The New York Ripper* (1982). Their US counterparts included George A. Romero with his *Dead* series (1968–), Wes Craven with *The Last House on the Left* (1972) and John Carpenter, who has remained one of the quintessential US cult filmmakers over the past 50 years.

More recently, the notion of cult filmmakers and cult films has become a slippery proposition. Whereas a director or film was once defined as cult by their peripheral appeal to mainstream tastes, the presence of infinite channels to view such work, social media's engagement with the Other and the commercialisation of the very idea of cult appeal make it difficult to distinguish between pretenders and the genuine article. Moreover, who is the arbiter of such distinctions? *Cult Filmmakers*, shining a light on just a handful of names, only highlights how problematic a canon of cult filmmakers can be.

Rather than offering an authoritative guide through a rich history of cult filmmaking, this book aims to be another voice in the conversation about cult cinema. The individuals featured represent a small number of filmmakers whose work might have found increasing popularity, but nevertheless remain distinct in their place within film history. And their status need not preclude widespread success. Like Zahler and Cosmatos, Quentin Tarantino has channelled the vision and spirit of many other cult filmmakers to imbue his own work with a similar spirit. Some might regard him as more of a parodist – the archetypal postmodern filmmaker in his assembling of a bricolage of tropes and genre elements – and not a genuine cult filmmaker. But *Reservoir Dogs* (1992) began its life as a cult film that happened to chime with the times – or mass audiences' tastes – and cemented the director's position as mainstream US cinema's 'cult' favourite. Other directors, such as David Cronenberg and Kathryn Bigelow, might have started out as cult directors, but the status now conferred on them is as iconoclasts at the heart of the mainstream film industry.

Bigelow remains a unique presence for her interest in the way violence interacts with cinema, an aspect often blithely accepted as existing solely in the domain of male filmmakers. But the image of the cult filmmaker has for too long been regarded within all too narrow boundaries. Widening the field makes for a far more interesting perspective, as proven in the work of the pioneering writer Pete Tombs, whose enthusiasm for all kinds of weird and wonderful cinema from around the world is infectious. Like Tarantino, Anna Biller revels in playing with genre, but her films also engage with the male gaze, offering up an alternative take on gender roles. Věra Chytilová employed a similar position with her extraordinary Czech New Wave breakthrough *Daisies* (1966). Furthermore, US society took on a very different identity in the films of Oscar Micheaux, who did more than most – and before Melvin Van Peebles and Gordon Parks – to present the experience of African Americans.

The scope of what constitutes a cult filmmaker needs to be increased further, far beyond the platform to which this collection of portraits remains limited. However, it is hoped that the profiles here contribute to widening the discussion of cult cinema past and present. It is difficult to see where the future of cult cinema lies and how it will evolve. As audiences have more access to older films and once-forgotten filmmakers are viewed in a different light, the canon of cult movies will likely shift. This may, in turn, influence the style of future cult titles. And there will always be taboos to challenge or breach and movies whose quality is no impediment to their enjoyment, along with those singular cinematic experiences whose very strangeness guarantees them a place among the great, good, bad and awful of the cult movie universe.

ANA LILY AMIRPOUR (1976)

— APOCALYPTIC VISIONARY

If there was ever a guidebook to becoming a cult filmmaker, one of its principal rules should be that a cult film needs to stand apart – be truly unique. This is what writer-director Ana Lily Amirpour achieves with her debut feature, which she describes as 'the first Iranian vampire spaghetti western'.

Born in the English coastal town of Margate, Amirpour's family moved to the United States when she was a child. She graduated in filmmaking from UCLA, and then directed a number of shorts, most notably *A Girl Walks Home Alone at Night* (2011), which became her feature debut in 2014.

Key to her two features is Amirpour's refusal to present female protagonists as hapless victims. The main characters in both her debut and her follow-up feature, *The Bad Batch* (2016), might not be fully in control of their situations, but they are resilient and intuitive enough to forge their own paths. As such, Amirpour turns the male-centric elements of exploitation cinema on their head.

Amirpour's cult appeal is underpinned by her association with Vice Films, which released both of her features, adding 'coolness' to her profile. To watch her debut is to see elements of the vampire and spaghetti western genres fused with the indie look of early Jim Jarmusch. It also echoes the emotionally glacial allure of other US indie filmmakers of the 1990s, such as Michael Almereyda and Hal Hartley: two directors who made the most of Elina Löwensohn, whose ethereal screen presence in their films is echoed by Sheila Vand as Amirpour's eponymous anti-heroine. By contrast, *The Bad Batch* plays out like a story unfolding in the same universe as Max Rockatansky, albeit minus the testosterone-fuelled vehicular carnage.

Music can often be the making of a cult film, and for both of her features Amirpour created a blend of the unknown and familiar. If Kiosk, Radio Tehran, Farah, and Free Electric Band are some of the lesser-known artists on the soundtrack for *A Girl*, *The Bad Batch* finds songs by Pantha du Prince and Die Antwoord alongside those by Darkside, Ace of Base and Culture Club. The music adds texture to Amirpour's imagery, which mostly exists without dialogue. The lack of substance has drawn criticism, but Amirpour's post-apocalyptic visions evince a command of genre elements that plays with conventions and challenges gender roles in exploitation cinema.

> **LUCIFER IS THE PATRON SAINT OF THE VISUAL ARTS. COLOUR, FORM – ALL THESE ARE THE WORK OF LUCIFER.**

KENNETH ANGER (1927)

Filmmaker, actor and questionable chronicler of Hollywood's seedier side, Kenneth Anger is known not only for his interest in the occult, but also for building a career that spearheaded the rise of homoerotic cinema.

Santa Monica-born Kenneth Wilbur Anglemyer entered cinema at an early age. His debut, *Ferdinand the Bull* (1937), was made when he was only ten years old, but Anger has subsequently dismissed the film and now regards his sophomore effort, *Who Has Been Rocking My Dreamboat* (1941), as his real entry into filmmaking. Made when he was 14, it was followed by *Prisoner of Mars* (1942), inspired by the Flash Gordon serials that were screening in cinemas at the time. Although these early films differ wildly from his later work, they reveal the director's enthusiasm for the short film form, which he maintained throughout his career.

Around the same time as these early shorts, Anger became fascinated with the occult and was introduced to the work of Aleister Crowley and his Thelema religion. The decision to fully integrate his beliefs into his filmmaking coincided with Anger discovering his homosexuality. These elements combined in his most famous – and notorious – series work, *Magick Lantern Cycle*. Made over a period of 34 years, it

began with the controversial *Fireworks* (1947). Upon this film's release, Anger was arrested on obscenity charges, and the case made its way to the California Supreme Court. There, the film was deemed to be art rather than pornography and the case was dismissed. By that time, *Fireworks* had a significant following and gave Anger prestige in the underground filmmaking world. One notable fan was the sexologist Alfred Kinsey.

Anger then moved to Paris and became friends with Jean Cocteau. However, funding proved problematic, and some projects took decades to complete. In the late 1950s, he returned to the United States and, in need of money, penned the first volume of his *Hollywood Babylon* series, a collection of stories charting the darker side of Hollywood's golden age. Alongside this, the shorts continued, including his masterpiece *Scorpio Rising* (1963), which drew inspiration from the nascent West Coast biker culture.

Anger's reputation has increased over the decades. His use of pre-recorded songs was innovative at one time, but is now a staple in mainstream cinema. A retrospective of his work at New York's Museum of Modern Art in 2009 was a testimony to his enduring influence as a filmmaker and visionary.

GREGG ARAKI   (1959)

—— THE ANTI-TASTEMAKER

Writer-director Gregg Araki's desire to shock with films that challenged societal norms made him the bad boy of the New Queer Cinema scene in the 1990s.

Born in Los Angeles, Araki has talked about how he immersed himself in classical Hollywood in his early years, before discovering that his interests lay in world cinema and in challenging the norms of mainstream filmmaking practices. It soon became clear that Araki would be aligned with the collection of US filmmakers who made up the New Queer Cinema that emerged in the late 1980s. However, as he shifted gear, from the no-to-low-budget early features *Three Bewildered People in the Night* (1987), *The Long Weekend* (1989) and *The Living End* (1992) to more propulsive, stylised films, the shock factor of his work made him one of the most controversial US filmmakers of the 1990s.

Araki's breakthrough films comprise teen dramas featuring attractive actors, pureposefully shallow dialogue, often extremely heightened emotions and driving soundtracks. However, they are a far cry from the comparatively innocent worlds of John Hughes' 1980s school movies, and different from the slacker lives portrayed in other youth-oriented US films of the period. Their form of rebellion entails a wholesale rejection of the values held dear by American society in favour of anarchy. Araki remains best known for his 'Teen Apocalypse Trilogy': *Totally F***ed Up* (1993), *The Doom Generation* (1995) and *Nowhere* (1997). They play out like a gut reaction to the Generation X films, with angst-ridden characters more likely to explode with violence than any that populate a Richard Linklater film. Violence in Araki's worlds is wildly over the top, even absurdist. In one famous scene from *The Doom Generation*, a bizarre moment follows the decapitation of of a gun-wielding convenience store owner. It is not so much that his head is blown clean off that makes the scene, but that it lands on a plate of fast food, reanimates, and regurgitates whatever snacks it has landed on. Even the disturbing climax of the film, featuring castration, sexual assault and mass murder, evinces an air of comic-book absurdity. Likewise, the pansexual adventures of a student in the outlandish sci-fi feature *Kaboom* (2010) are a stark contrast to most US dramas set in a college.

Although his films are often referred to as kitsch and nihilistic, Araki himself has resisted such descriptions. His preference is to look at his body of work as a series of outsider tales. Whether his characters are gay, straight or queer, his interest lies in telling stories outside the norm. If his early work rages against a nation belatedly coming to terms with the impact of AIDS (in *The Living End*, one character suggests: 'Why don't we go to Washington and blow Bush's brains out!'), Araki's more recent work, such as his most acclaimed and

successful features *Mysterious Skin* (2004) and *White Bird in a Blizzard* (2014), clearly point to his maturing as a filmmaker. His singularly take on teen life has made him the go-to director for youth-oriented TV dramas such as *Riverdale*, *Heather* and *13 Reasons Why*.

DARREN ARONOFSKY (1969)

—— MAINSTREAM REBEL

Writer-director Darren Aronofsky's career has been uncompromising in its vision, and has seen him progress from the periphery of independent cinema to the heart of mainstream blockbuster filmmaking.

No one watches an Aronofsky film for an easy time. The filmmaker exists within a small band of directors who have made a film budgeted at over $100 million dollars without sacrificing their vision. And that vision is often dark, tortured and edging towards the apocalyptic.

A student of the American Film Institute, where his graduate film *Supermarket Sweep* (1991) was universally acclaimed, Aronofsky won the Best Director award at the Sundance Film Festival for his feature debut, *Pi* (1998). Drawing on mathematical theories, Kabbalah, the Torah and the Koran, and driven by kinetic camerawork and Clint Mansell's mesmerising score, *Pi* is in equal parts riveting and disturbing. The filmmaker went further with his nightmarish follow-up, *Requiem for a Dream* (2000). Adapting Hubert Selby Jr.'s tale of narcotic and opiate addiction, Aronofsky interweaves his four characters' stories into a bleak tapestry of lives destroyed by drugs. Mansell's 'Lux Aeterna', with its stabbing strings, makes for a breathtaking accompaniment, but, brilliant as it is, the film is one that only

those with the most hardened disposition can watch repeatedly.

If a cult film is defined as a work that teeters on the precipice of the ridiculous, leaving most audiences baffled, bemused or enraged, Aronofsky hit the bullseye with *The Fountain* (2006). A triptych of tales featuring Hugh Jackman and Rachel Weisz, told in the past, present and future, it appears stranger now than it did on its initial release. Its premise, regarding the search for the tree of life, told through the prism of interconnected love stories, is merely a platform for a series of extraordinary set pieces that might make no sense, but look magnificent. And yet, Aronofsky's ongoing fascination with obsessive characters shines through.

That film failed spectacularly at the box office, and Aronofsky's subsequent films, *The Wrestler* (2008), *Black Swan* (2010), and even *Noah* (2014), suggested that the filmmaker had curbed his wilder excesses. But then he delivered his strangest film yet with *Mother!* (2017). It can be viewed as an allegory of a despoiled Eden, a warning of the imminent danger we are wreaking upon the environment. Love it or loathe it, the film cements Aronofsky's status as the preeminent cult US filmmaker of the 21st century.

66 IN A HORROR FILM, LIGHTING IS 70% OF THE EFFECTIVENESS. IT'S ESSENTIAL IN CREATING THE ATMOSPHERE. 99

MARIO BAVA   (1914–1980)

— GIALLO INNOVATOR

A gifted cinematographer who turned to directing, Mario Bava worked across various genres, but is most closely associated with a particular strain of Italian horror film.

Born in San Remo, Italy, he was the son of Eugenio Bava, a noted special-effects photographer. He cut his teeth as a cinematographer for Roberto Rossellini in the early 1940s, and his skill with lighting made him a popular choice to work with stars including Gina Lollobrigida and Aldo Fabrizi.

Image is everything in the films that Bava shot, as well as those he would eventually direct. A perfectly constructed shadow or a dash of colour could alter the tone, add suspense or embellish upon a specific theme. Bava became a master of atmosphere, but he was initially known as the dependable go-to technician who could add magic to a production. He once told an interviewer that films are 'a magician's forge' and what attracted him to them was the idea of being 'presented with a problem and being able to solve it. Nothing else; just to create an illusion, and effect, with almost nothing'. It is an approach that served him well. His status in Italian cinema by the mid-1950s was such that he was promoted from cinematographer to director when filmmaker Riccardo Freda walked out on *The Devil's Commandment* (1957), generally regarded as the first Italian horror film. He was an uncredited director on several films around this period, and also produced special effects for what would become the popular Italian sword-and-sandals genre. However, it wasn't until *Black Sunday* (1960) that he was finally credited as sole director.

Throughout his career, Bava moved between genres as varied as science fiction (*Planet of the Vampires*, 1965), comic book adaptation (*Danger: Diabolik*, 1968) and soft-core sex comedy (*Four Times That Night*, 1971). But he achieved fame with his horror films. In particular, he popularised the giallo film, which blended thriller and horror tropes, along with a touch of eroticism, to create a style of film that was common in Italian cinema from the 1960s to the 1980s. *Black Sunday* set the standard, but the addition of colour in films such as *Blood and Black Lace* (1964) and *Kill, Baby ... Kill!* (1966) highlighted Bava's baroque style. His extraordinary work rate notwithstanding – he directed/codirected 24 films in 18 years – Bava's importance as a filmmaker has stretched far beyond the genre he came to dominate.

KATHRYN BIGELOW (1951)

— ACTION MAESTRO

Eschewing lazy gender stereotyping, Kathryn Bigelow has risen to the front rank of action movie directors by finding a perfect balance between exploiting and deconstructing the genre.

A chameleon who has successfully reinvented herself several times as a filmmaker, Bigelow was born in San Carlos, California, but moved to New York after attending the San Francisco Art Institute. A member of a study programme at the Whitney Museum of American Art, she became firmly established in the city's art world, befriending Julian Schnabel, undertaking apprenticeships with Richard Serra and Lawrence Weiner and – a little more tangentially – entering the real estate world with acclaimed composer Philip Glass.

After a few years, Bigelow shifted towards film, signing up to Columbia University's MFA film programme and teaching part time at CalArts. Her graduation short, *The Set-Up* (1978), presaged the preoccupations of her early features. Footage of two men fighting – shot over one night, she asked her actors to make actual physical contact with their punches – unfolds as the voice of two academics discuss the meaning of what is shown. Violence became central to Bigelow's films, and controversy has surrounded the way she employs it. Although she has never identified herself as an explicitly female or feminist filmmaker, some critics have taken umbrage with a woman directing such explicitly violent films. Most notoriously, a rape scene in Bigelow's *Strange Days* (1995) attracted significant opprobrium from a number of critics. It shows two characters wearing devices that allow each to experience the sensation of victim and assailant – an attempt to question

the way sexual violence is represented on the screen.

Near Dark (1987) remains one of the most original takes on the vampire myth: the film is located in the heart of Texas, with the vampires portrayed as a band of misfits. It revealed Bigelow's skill at staging complex set pieces, which only increased in scale with her action trilogy *Blue Steel* (1990), *Point Break* (1991) and *Strange Days*. Of the three, *Point Break*'s perfect balance of testosterone-driven thrills and healthy cynicism towards macho-oriented culture remains the best known, but all three found Bigelow challenging assumptions about gender or race, the latter explored through a Rodney King-like scenario in *Strange Days*, which may have arrived in cinemas a little too early for audiences after the actual events that prompted the LA riots.

If *Strange Days*' failure at the box office stalled Bigelow's career for a number of years, her triumphant return with *The Hurt Locker* (2009) transformed her fortunes in the industry. She became the first female to win a Best Director Oscar and has since forged a path directing films based on controversial moments in recent US history. Her fascination with how violence is portrayed remains, albeit presented with more elan and lacking the wilder spirit that made her earlier films so compelling in their balance of technical brilliance and devil-may-care spirit.

THERE SHOULD BE
MORE WOMEN DIRECTING;
I THINK THERE'S JUST NOT
THE AWARENESS THAT IT'S
REALLY POSSIBLE.

ANNA BILLER

No colour is too kitsch in writer, director, producer, editor, designer, composer and actor Anna Biller's retro-fitted worlds.

Recent years have seen a small number of contemporary filmmakers focusing on reviving and reinventing tropes of continental European genre films from the 1960s and 1970s: Peter Strickland, Hélène Cattet and Bruno Forzani among them. In comparison, Biller's work may seem tame, revelling more in pastiche than full-blooded thrills. But her contributions successfully engage with gender stereotypes past and present, offering a playful and knowing take on an era whose genre cinema frequently revelled in regressive gender stereotypes and misogyny.

Biller's body of work remains small – four shorts and two features across two decades – but her investment in her productions betrays an acute eye for exacting detail. Born in Los Angeles, Biller studied art at UCLA before graduating with an MFA in art and film from CalArts. Shortly after, she embarked on a series of shorts that defined her style. Identifying herself as a feminist, Biller has spoken about her interest in inserting the female gaze into her work while overturning tropes regarding male-female relationships. She took on the key craft roles for these early films, a style of working that has continued with her two features.

Viva (2007) initially recalls a 1970s-style sexploitation film. But whereas female characters were little more than the object of male desire in those original films, Biller has them take control: both dominating and driving the narrative. Playing out like the LSD-infused love child of colour-era Douglas Sirk and Jess Franco at his most lascivious, *Viva* balances cine literacy with retro charm, creating a singularly strange genre hybrid. It stood outside anything released in the United States at the time and presaged the retro styling of more recent filmmakers.

The Love Witch (2016) opened a few days after Donald Trump won the US presidential election. It was perfect timing for Biller, whose film represents the antithesis of everything the president-elect stood for. At the same time, Biller managed to outdo the outrageousness of *Viva* in almost every way. In this tale of a witch who destroys men by unleashing their true emotional potential, her costumes are a vivid rainbow of pastel shades, complimented by equally outrageous production design that takes the late 1960s and early 1970s as its inspiration. As politics in the United States has taken a more conservative turn, particularly in the arena of gender identity, Biller's work seems all the more relevant.

LIZZIE BORDEN (1958)

—— FEMINIST CRUSADER

Although her output is small, Lizzie Borden's importance as a filmmaker is defined by her pioneering work in furthering the feminist cause in cinema.

Feminist science fiction might not be the most populous of genres, but in Borden's *Born in Flames* (1983) it has its radical manifesto. It is a film created out of the filmmaker's observations of a patriarchal society, where the subjugation of women is the norm.

Linda Elizabeth Borden chose to take the name of the 19th century Massachusetts murderer when she was 11 years old, partly as an act of rebellion towards her parents. She studied art at Wellesley College near Boston, where she first became directly involved in gender politics and feminist debates. After initially deciding on a life as a fine artist, her exposure to Jean-Luc Godard's films changed the trajectory of her career. Her first film, *Regrouping* (1976), focused on the varying success of two collectives of female artists, raising questions about their role in society and its attitude towards them. Although the film highlighted Borden's distinctive voice, it was almost a decade before her groundbreaking second film surfaced.

Born in Flames was subject to a major retrospective tour in 2017: perfect timing for a film that seemed to respond directly to the controversy surrounding President Trump's comments about, and attitude towards, women. Its re-emergence in cinemas was a bleak reminder of how much remained to be done in terms of race, gender and media representation in US society and beyond. Filmed over five years and at a cost of $30,000, it was a 'one day in the future' tale of women revolting against a tide of misogyny. Borden originally intended to offer a white female perspective, but expanded the film's range and political scope to take on racial politics. Although reviews were initially mixed, the film is now seen as a classic of feminist cinema and a key cultural text.

Borden's career has since been varied. *Working Girls* (1986) is a powerful portrait of sex workers, some of whom had appeared in her previous film and had inspired the filmmaker's exploration of the topic of prostitution with rare intelligence and sensitivity. More recently, her involvement in film has been developing projects that are yet to be realised and script doctoring on other people's films. However, renewed interest in *Born in Flames* may offer Borden an opportunity to once again achieve her ambitions on the screen.

TIM BURTON (1958)

— HOLLYWOOD FANTASIST

A former Disney animator-turned-director, Tim Burton saw his offbeat vision of the world transformed into mainstream success.

It is not difficult to believe that, in his youth, Burton might have been like Sid Phillips, who mangles and mutates his toys beyond recognition in *Toy Story* (1995). But from Burton's perspective, Sid was not the cruel torturer that Woody and friends believed him to be. He was in fact his toy's liberator, incorporating them into his own world vision. The resulting creatures might be anathema to the ethos of *Toy Story*, but they highlight the darker recesses to which a child's imagination can journey and might be the same point from which Burton's own cinematic musings began.

Burton grew up in Burbank, a stone's throw from Hollywood and not dissimilar to the almost pathologically ordered pastel environment the filmmaker captured in *Edward Scissorhands* (1990). Once again, it is possible to see a little of the youthful Burton in one of his most fully realised creations: the eponymous hero who will never fit into this world. In his teens, Burton was a square peg forced to fit into the round hole that was the US education system. But his private passion for filmmaking carried on unabated by his academic shortcomings. He attended CalArts, and his short *Stalk of the Celery Monster* (1979) attracted the attention of Walt Disney Animated Studios. It was in the era before the studio had successfully rejuvenated its image and Burton was a storyboard and concept artist for *The Fox and the Hound* (1981), *Tron* (1982), and *The Black Cauldron* (1985). He also produced *Vincent* (1982) and *Frankenweenie* (1984), whose dark tone was apposite to Disney's worldview and resulted in Burton being fired.

But the images that Burton created soon attracted supporters, including Paul Rubens, who saw in Burton the perfect director to transport his popular television character Pee-wee Herman onto the big screen. *Pee-wee's Big Adventure* (1985) led the way to the dark and delirious fever dream of the black comedy *Beetlejuice* (1988). Like *Batman* (1989), *Edward Scissorhands*, *Batman Returns* (1992) and *Ed Wood* (1994), it was a film of singular vision, defining Burton as a visual stylist par excellence. In his youth, Burton might have created art that existed on the fringes of society, but as a filmmaker at the height of his creativity, he succeeded in drawing huge audiences into his strange worlds, where freaks and outsiders are the norm.

JOHN CARPENTER (1948)

—— MASTER OF GENRE

Director, screenwriter and composer John Carpenter helped define genre cinema as much as he paid homage to earlier pioneers.

Few US genre directors have mined their passion for cinema and the filmmakers they most admire as much as Carpenter. His cinema, primarily horror and science fiction, pushes genre boundaries while acknowledging his debt to directors from previous generations, either through pastiche or remake. In turn, his own body of work has proven influential over subsequent filmmakers.

Carpenter was obsessed with film from a young age, producing shorts before he began high school. In particular, he was fascinated by the classical Hollywood western, as practised by John Ford and Howard Hawks, whose *Rio Bravo* (1959) Carpenter would reimagine as an urban siege fought between cops and street gangs in his sophomore feature *Assault on*

Precinct 13 (1976). He attended USC School of Cinema-Television in 1969, where he produced the acclaimed shorts *Captain Voyeur* (1969), whose stalking narrative predates *Halloween* (1978), and *The Resurrection of Broncho Billy* (1970), which won an Academy Award for Best Live Action Short Film.

Carpenter's approach to filmmaking has always mirrored the methods of his cinematic heroes, who were expected to work within budget and on time. His debut, *Dark Star* (1974), failed in this respect – although it remains a marvel of ultra-low budget filmmaking and has proven hugely influential over subsequent science fiction action films such as *Star Wars: Episode IV—A New Hope* (1977) – and so Carpenter has often cited *Assault on Precinct 13* as his first film proper. Outside of his signature haunting synth scores, almost all of which he composed, Carpenter's filmmaking style

❝ I MADE A DECISION BACK IN 1978 THAT, IN A TRADE OFF FOR MONEY WHEN I DIRECTED HALLOWEEN, I WOULD HAVE MY NAME ABOVE THE TITLE IN ORDER TO BASICALLY BRAND THESE MOVIES MY OWN. **❞**

has employed the use of Steadicam and limited light sources. He has also been a proponent of a larger, anamorphic aspect ratio. All of his films, with the exception of *Dark Star* and *The Ward* (2010), were shot on widescreen. He is also known for working with a regular ensemble of actors, from lesser known supporting actors such as Charles Cyphers, Peter Jason and George 'Buck' Flower to star Kurt Russell, who played the lead in five of his films.

Carpenter is arguably one of the greatest cult filmmakers to work in Hollywood, albeit on its periphery. He had great commercial success with *Halloween*, *The Fog* (1980), *Escape from New York* (1981) and *Starman* (1984), but many other projects initially failed to win over audiences. However, like many great cult films, a number of Carpenter's 'failures' now have a significant following. *The Thing* (1982), another homage to a Howard Hawks film (*The Thing from Another World*, 1951), is a classic update of the monster movie, with groundbreaking special effects, while *Big Trouble in Little China* (1986) is a gleefully silly mash-up of various genres. The media and political satire of *They Live* (1988) seems more prescient than ever, and *In the Mouth of Madness* (1994), a Lovecraftian horror homage and the third instalment in the director's *Apocalypse* trilogy after *The Thing* and *Prince of Darkness* (1987), is a manic and mordantly funny delight.

PARK CHAN-WOOK (1963)

—— VOICE OF VENGEANCE

Revenge might be a dish best served cold, but in writer-director Park Chan-wook's celebrated *Vengeance* trilogy, it is presented at sub-zero temperatures.

Born in Seoul, South Korea, Park created a lauded and popular body of work that refashions the mechanics of genre cinema. His subject matter may often be pitch black and his unwillingness to shy away from gruesome acts of violence bold, but his style is never less than sophisticated. The sheen of his work is matched by the complexity of its narratives, whose themes encompass guilt, desire, loyalty and trust.

Park's star rose with what became known as New Korean Cinema, comprising a group of filmmakers who profited from film investment before the Asian financial collapse of 1997. By the end of the 1990s, they were delivering glossy, Hollywood-style films with an Asia-centric spin. Park's feature debut, *Saminjo* (1997), was popular domestically, but it was *Joint Security Area* (2000) that raised his profile internationally. A slick thriller set at the border between North and South Korea, it not only provided thrills, but also underpinned Park's innate ability to offer up mainstream genre entertainment while probing complex, often morally ambiguous terrain.

If violence and sex are a mainstay in much of Park's work, it is never solely for audiences' gratification. He applies an equal moral weight to both, and implies that actions – consensual or forced – always come at a cost. Nowhere is this more apparent than in the *Vengeance* trilogy: *Sympathy for Mr Vengeance* (2002), *Oldboy* (2003) and *Lady Vengeance* (2005). In each, characters come to understand innately the universal aspect of Newton's third law that every action has an equal and opposite reaction. Like his subsequent films, Park's *Vengeance* trilogy eschews the moral vacuity of many a Hollywood action film or thriller, whereby the hero is exempt from judgment as a result of their deeds. The violence is bloody and shocking, acknowledging the vicarious pleasures of screen violence: a scene in *Oldboy* that features the anti-hero armed with nothing but a hammer and facing an onslaught of adversaries is undeniably thrilling. However, it never shies away from the damage such a sequence inflicts on a body.

Subsequent films *Thirst* (2009), a starkly original take on the vampire myth, and the erotic period thriller *The Handmaiden* (2016) have cemented Park's position as one of the most compelling contemporary directors. But his *Vengeance* trilogy ensured his status as a cult filmmaker and unique voice in cinema.

BENJAMIN CHRISTENSEN (1879–1959)

⸺ WITCHCRAFT CHRONICLER

Benjamin Christensen's reputation and fame is based entirely on his startling and unconventional third feature as a filmmaker: *Häxan* (1922).

Born in the Danish city of Viborg, actor and director Christensen originally studied medicine before being bitten by the acting bug. He auditioned for the Danish Royal Theatre in 1901 and made his screen debut in 1911. Almost nothing remains of Christensen's work from this period, but in 1913 he took over a film-production company and made his directorial feature debut with *The Mysterious X* (1914). Ostensibly a spy drama, the film is remarkable for Christensen's creative and technical prowess, already signalling a filmmaker with a desire to push the boundaries of the medium.

Christensen intermittently returned to acting, both on stage and screen. His most notable role was as the artist Claude Zoret in Danish filmmaker Carl Theodor Dreyer's landmark gay drama *Michael* (1924). Shot in Germany, the film was followed by two undistinguished productions directed by Christensen, who was then offered a chance to work for MGM. He joined countless other émigrés working in Hollywood, but his experiences were uneven at best. He had some success

with a vehicle for star Norma Shearer, but *Mockery* (1927), which featured Lon Chaney and was set against the backdrop of the Russian Revolution, was an unmitigated critical disaster. He moved to Warner Brothers, where he produced a crime drama and three horror films, but his love affair with Tinseltown had eroded and he moved back to Denmark in 1929. After ten years directing for the stage, Christensen returned to filmmaking with the surprise success *Children of Divorce* (1939). Two more features followed, but the failure of the spy thriller *Lady with the Light Gloves* (1942) ended his film career.

Christensen's place in cinema history is assured by *Häxan*. A four-part study of the nature of witchcraft and superstition, the film was based on three years of intensive study by Christensen into necromancy. *Häxan* is ostensibly a documentary, but Christensen dabbled in fictional recreations of witchcraft practices and experimented with form, pushing the film into the terrain of horror. Though popular in Denmark and Sweden, establishing Christensen as his country's most important filmmaker after Dreyer, the film's depiction of sex and death saw it censored heavily internationally, which has only helped bolster its status as a bona fide cult classic.

VĚRA CHYTILOVÁ (1929-2014)

—— NEW WAVE MISCHIEF-MAKER

One of the key members of the Czech New Wave, Věra Chytilová is best known for a madcap satire whose mayhem offers up a scathing portrait of communist rule.

Born in Prague, Chytilová spent all her professional life identifying as an individual. She may have been grouped with the Czech New Wave because of her anti-establishment satires and labelled a feminist for her stance against patriarchy in all areas of Czech society, but when questioned she insisted that she was very much her own person. It is a sentiment that is present throughout her work, whose themes might align with larger artistic or social movements, and is extraordinary for its level of innovation and invention.

After initially studying architecture and philosophy, Chytilová abandoned them in favour of the fashion world. She entered the film industry as a clapper-board operator at Prague's Barrandov Studios. An application to study film there was rejected, so she applied to, and was accepted by, FAMU, the Czech capital's other film school. She produced two acclaimed shorts while there – *Ceiling* (1961) and *A Bag of Fleas* (1962) – before directing her first commercial feature, *Something Different* (1963), which contrasts the lives of a gymnast and a housewife, highlighting the destructive nature of patriarchal standards. However, it was her second feature, *Daisies* (1966), that not only proved to be Chytilová's breakthrough, but also the film that would define her entire career.

Ostensibly a knockabout comedy following two young women, Marie I and Marie II (non-professional actors Jitka Cerhová and Ivana Karbanová), *Daisies* offers up a caustic broadside against the communist establishment and its hypocritical ruling elite. The thesis behind the series of increasingly outrageous

escapades is that if the world has gone bad, then why shouldn't two of its citizens. Culminating in an epic food fight in a banqueting hall that is prepared and reserved for party members – the waste of food in this scene is one of the reasons given for officials banning the film – *Daisies* is unrelenting in its social critique. And while her characters refuse to play to any normal standards of behaviour, Chytilová employs a barrage of stylistic effects for each scene, from filters and different speed film to a variety of editing techniques, to disorient and challenge audiences. It is an approach that the filmmaker continued in her subsequent feature, *Fruit of Paradise* (1970), and one that made *Daisies* a pivotal work among those by Czech New Wave filmmakers, who stood opposed to the censorial dictates of Soviet rule.

Chytilová directed 16 features in her lifetime. Describing herself as 'an overheated kettle that you can't turn down', her unwillingness to parry to ideological, political, societal or moral conventions found her in a constant battle with authorities in the Soviet-controlled film industry. But she refused to leave Czechoslovakia, even after the 1968 invasion, preferring to stay and fight for her individual rights. This came at a cost and for years she could not find work. When she did, from the late 1970s on and until her final film *Pleasant Memories* (2006), her filmmaking style became calmer, adopting a more conventional visual approach. However, the themes of her work continued to articulate her sense of outrage at the way women were treated in Czech society, before and after Soviet rule.

❝ YOU ALWAYS HAVE TO
WORK AS IF WHAT YOU'RE
WORKING ON COULD
BE YOUR LAST. **❞**

SOFIA COPPOLA (1971)

—— INDIE QUEEN

After a short-lived acting career, Sofia Coppola worked her way to the front rank of US filmmakers with a body of work that is noted for its aesthetic qualities.

The daughter of Francis Ford Coppola, Sofia played the infant in the baptism scene in the climax of *The Godfather* (1972) and, more infamously, Michael Corleone's daughter in *The Godfather Part III* (1990). Her performance in that film was mostly derided by critics but she had never wanted to act, preferring a life behind the camera. A year before the final *Godfather* entry, she cowrote the screenplay for *Life Without Zöe*, one-third of the portmanteau film *New York Stories* (1989). The tale of a young girl who lives a privileged life in an opulent hotel, it was made a decade before her feature debut but hints at themes that became common throughout her work, from the impressive *The Virgin Suicides* (1999) through to her female-empowered version of *The Beguiled* (2017).

After ten years working in the fashion industry, as well as making music videos and a clutch of shorts, Coppola debuted with a seductive, visually entrancing adaptation of Jeffrey Eugenides' book *The Virgin Suicides* (1993). The film's entrancing visuals, employing soft hues to evoke a bygone era, and to add weight to the ultimate actions of the Lisbon sisters, not only announced Coppola as a major new filmmaking talent, but also hinted at the style she would develop with her work. Predominantly focusing on female protagonists, Coppola's films explore female representation, both past and present, often challenging stereotypes. They also examine the nature of celebrity, particularly in the way she employs visuals as a brittle superficiality masking the reality of people's lives. As such, there isn't a huge stretch between court life in *Marie Antoinette* (2006) and contemporary Los Angeles in *The Bling Ring* (2013).

Although aspects of Coppola's life can be seen to inform elements of *Life Without Zöe* and *Somewhere* (2010), *Lost in Translation* (2003) arguably remains the filmmaker's most autobiographical feature. An account of a young woman who befriends a cynical actor in a hotel in Tokyo, it is believed to be loosely inspired by Coppola's marriage to Spike Jonze. But what it achieves, beyond the Oscar Coppola won for her original screenplay and an audience that has grown with each subsequent film, is a sense of wonder at the world. Along with *The Virgin Suicides*, it defined Coppola as a singular voice in modern cinema.

ROGER CORMAN   (1926)

In addition to his credits as a director, producer, occasional writer and actor, Roger Corman was responsible for encouraging a generation of filmmakers who came to dominate the US cinematic landscape.

Corman directed 50 films between 1955 and 1969, plus a handful more up to his final feature, *Roger Corman's Frankenstein Unbound* (1990). But this figure pales against the 400-odd features – and counting – he produced for both cinema and television over a 60-year career. Few have been quite so prolific; nor has anyone supported the nascent careers of such a rich generation of filmmakers, which includes Martin Scorsese, Francis Ford Coppola, Jonathan Demme and Ron Howard, among others. The films they made with Corman might lack the prestige or elan of their greatest successes, but he allowed them to cut their teeth on genre films, offering the invaluable experience of working on a film set and indulging them to experiment with the medium.

The 'Pope of Pop Cinema', as he became known, was born in Detroit, Michigan. He studied engineering at Stanford University and English at Oxford University before spending time in Paris. He sold his first script, *Highway Dragnet* (1954), for

$12,000, which he used to fund his first feature as producer, *Monster from the Ocean Floor* (1954). With its outrageous title and B-movie production values, it set the standard for the films Corman would produce over the next decade. Occasionally, the titles were the only good quality of a film, but regard for Corman's oeuvre gradually improved. *Machine-Gun Kelly* (1958) received positive notices, and his series of Edgar Allen Poe adaptations in the 1960s, which includes *House of Usher* (1960), *The Pit and the Pendulum* (1961), *The Raven* (1963) and *The Masque of the Red Death* (1964), along with countercultural classics such as *The Trip* (1967), remain high points in his career.

Corman's body of work is so vast, it is best regarded in its entirety. He was the youngest filmmaker to be given a retrospective at the Cinémathèque Française, and both the British Film Institute and New York's Museum of Modern Art followed suit. His encouragement of the film careers of so many great directors was repaid with roles in their films, from Francis Ford Coppola's *The Godfather: Part II* (1974) and Ron Howard's *Apollo 13* (1995) to Jonathan Demme's *The Silence of the Lambs* (1991) and *Philadelphia* (1993).

ALEX COX (1954)

— INDIE OUTSIDER

A cinephile whose films evince a rough-at-the-edges punk aesthetic, Alex Cox is the ultimate cult auteur and a champion of world cinema.

Originally a law student at Oxford University, Cheshire-born Cox moved to Bristol to study film, before winning a Fulbright Scholarship to UCLA. He formed the production company City Edge Productions with the intention of funding his screenplay *Repo Man*. Instead, he attracted the attention of former The Monkees guitarist Michael Nesmith, who took his project to Universal Studios and secured a budget of $1 million for a film that Cox thought would cost $70,000. *Repo Man* (1984) was not an immediate success, but it managed to secure a re-release at a cinema in New York, where it played for 18 months, finally earning $4 million. Cult appeal partly lay in the soundtrack, but there is also the combination of Harry Dean Stanton and Emilio Estevez's odd-couple relationship and the film's utter strangeness.

Cox travelled further down the punk rabbit hole with his biopic *Sid & Nancy* (1986) and the road-movie-cum-western *Straight to Hell* (1987). If Cox's style with these early films was steadfastly low-fi, eschewing Hollywood slickness for a graininess that gave his films a sense of anarchy, he upped his game with *Walker* (1987), an admirable attempt to document the life of William Walker, an American 'filibuster' who attempted to wrestle control of Nicaragua away from its national leaders. But its outspoken left-wing politics, Brechtian approach to drama and the critical drubbing that ensued ensured it was Cox's last 'Hollywood' production.

Cox's subsequent career as a director careened between ultra-low-budget productions such as *Repo Chick* (2009), a series of television dramas and the Mexican police procedural *Highway Patrolman* (1991). He has also been a champion of cinema history, refusing to draw a line between high and low art. His books *10,000 Ways to Die* (2009), *The President and the Provocateur: The Parallel Lives of JFK and Lee Harvey Oswald* (2013) and *Alex Cox's Introduction to Film: A Director's Perspective* (2016) underpin his passion for engaging audiences in discussions about film. Arguably his greatest impact in this respect was as the host of television show *Moviedrome* (1988–1994), which saw him introduce a wide variety of films, encouraging audiences to pay as much attention to exploitation cinema as they would to more serious, critically acclaimed titles. For a generation of filmmakers such as Ben Wheatley and Edgar Wright, Cox made them want to make their own mark in cinema.

DAVID CRONENBERG   (1943)

—— BODY HORROR SPECIALIST

From body horror to scathing satire, David Cronenberg's work is a battlefield between the body and mind, frequently shocking and often mordantly funny.

At some point, Cronenberg, who was born in Toronto, became established. No longer the filmmaker whose early work saw him accused of being a pariah of the Canadian film industry and whose 'sick' films should have seen him institutionalised, recent films such as *Crash* (1996), *A History of Violence* (2005) and *Maps to the Stars* (2014) have been feted by critics and played in competition at major festivals. Perhaps the change came with the commercial successes of *Scanners* (1981), *The Dead Zone* (1983) and the breakout hit *The Fly* (1986). Yet those films, like the subsequent *Dead Ringers* (1988), *Naked Lunch* (1991) and more recent work, still have the power to shock. Through them all is a probing exploration

of the human psyche and its impact upon the physical self. If later films differ in any way from his earlier work, the reason lies in Cronenberg expanding his interest beyond the corporeal.

After two celebrated medium-length films, *Stereo* (1969) and *Crimes of the Future* (1970), Cronenberg wrote and directed *Shivers* (1975). Also known as *The Parasite Murders*, *They Came from Within* and the overly literal *Orgy of the Blood Parasites*, Cronenberg's feature debut remains an unsettling examination of sexual promiscuity run amok in a state-of-the-art residential block. *Rabid* (1977) continued the theme of the infected body, albeit on a city scale, as an operation on a young woman who survives a road accident transforms her into a virus-infecting carrier. As with the subsequent *The Brood* (1979), these early features were a stark contrast to much of the horror being produced at

> **" CENSORS TEND TO DO WHAT ONLY PSYCHOTICS DO: THEY CONFUSE REALITY WITH ILLUSION. "**

the time. They could not be written off as merely gory entertainments – Cronenberg's preoccupations were too radical. His examination of contemporary society and its ills, manifested in the physical transformation of his characters, unsettled many critics and would continue to do so in later films, such as *Dead Ringers*, *Crash* and *Maps to the Stars*. But arguably no other film in Cronenberg's canon has continued to seem as relevant as *Videodrome* (1983): his exploration of the way media – both the message and the medium – can affect our lives.

After the startling head-exploding excess but narrative linearity of *Scanners* (1981), *Videodrome* arrived as something of a head-scratcher. What initially appears to be a thriller that delves into the murky world of violent porn soon becomes a surreal portrait of the way television has come to dominate our culture. A film that

mainlines William Burroughs, J.G. Ballard and the theories of Marshall McLuhan, *Videodrome* suggests that the medium is not so much a massage as a carcinogen, as it follows James Woods' sleazy television producer on a journey into an alternate reality. Increasingly incoherent as its protagonist becomes enmeshed in a nefarious world on the other side of the television screen, *Videodrome* finds Cronenberg at his delirious best.

CLAIRE DENIS (1946)

—— POST-COLONIAL PROVOCATEUR

Writer-director Claire Denis has forged a career that balances highbrow interpretations of literary classics with startling reinventions of popular genres.

Outsider status is a key element in all of Denis' work, whether it is a child's-eye view of colonial life in Africa, a Foreign Legion sergeant facing court martial at a remote outpost, a serial killer or vampire on the streets of Paris or the subject of a bizarre sexual experiment in outer space. Running through them all is Denis' eye for exacting detail, her rigorous intelligence in probing her characters' lives and the intensity of the situations in which she places them. She is regarded as one of the most challenging and accomplished contemporary filmmakers, utterly uncompromising in her vision of the world.

Born in Paris, Denis grew up in West Africa, where her father was a civil servant. Her experiences there are most clearly present in films such as the semi-autobiographical *Chocolat* (1988) and *White Material* (2009). She studied filmmaking at Le Fémis, after which she gained experience as an assistant director, first with Dušan Makavejev on his hugely controversial *Sweet Movie* (1974), then with Costa-Gavras, Jim Jarmusch and Wim Wenders, most notably on *Paris,*

Texas (1984) and *Wings of Desire* (1987). She debuted with *Chocolat* the following year, which was nominated for the top prize at the Cannes Film Festival. A tale of a young girl's experiences growing up in a French African colony, it proved to be a fascinating journey that Denis would further explore in *White Material* (2009). Africa was also the location of Denis' extraordinary *Beau Travail* (2000), which relocated Herman Melville's *Billy Budd* (1924) to a French Foreign Legion outpost in Djibouti. That film highlighted the director's penchant for long takes and also the time she takes editing, often re-ordering shots.

Although Denis' work eschews any simple genre categorisation – 1994's *I Can't Sleep* might be a profile of a serial killer but it could not be less like a conventional serial killer thriller – *Trouble Every Day* (2001) and *High Life* (2018) play out within the universe of the vampire and science-fiction movie. But both are far more studied and alienating in their engagement with corporeality, employing familiar motifs as a way of subverting rather than rigidly abiding to the strictures of a genre. The results, like her early, unclassifiable *No Fear, No Die* (1990), have cemented Denis' position as a filmmaker with a unique perspective on the way we live our lives.

AMAT ESCALANTE (1979)

—— VIOLENT VISIONARY

From the violence of an unending drug war to visitations from other worlds, writer, director and producer Amat Escalante offers uncompromising portraits of modern life.

Born in Barcelona, Escalante spent much of his youth in the central Mexican state of Guanajuato before returning to Spain to study film editing and sound design. After completing a further filmmaking course at the International School of Film and Television in Havana and directing his short *Amarrados* (2002), Escalante assisted fellow Mexican filmmaker Carlos Reygadas on *Battle in Heaven* (2005). The two became friends, and Reygadas' production company supported Escalante's nascent career as a director. While his debut *Sangre* (2005), a study in jealousy and states of ennui in long-term relationships, betrayed the participation of Reygadas, *Los Bastardos* (2008) saw the filmmaker develop his own style, balancing considerable technical skill with an increased dynamism. The film's escalating violence also presaged the more formally austere *Heli* (2013). In all three works, Escalante featured mainly non-professional actors, a muted palette and a preference for long takes.

Escalante's second and third features offer contrasting representations of Mexico, its diaspora, and the problems of alienation, class and crime. Both films are bleak portraits of characters caught up in a spiralling world of violence, but they refute a simplistic Trumpian take on the situation. Their nihilism might have attracted opprobrium and the violence criticism for its extremity, but Escalante highlights the helplessness of characters forced against their better judgment into situations from which there is no happy escape.

Escalante defines himself as an international rather than Mexican filmmaker, and his influences range from austere Belgian director Bruno Dumont to US experimental filmmaker James Benning. Although *The Untamed* (2016) evinces themes explored in his earlier work and is once again set in Mexico, the shift in genre – from crime to science fiction – gives it a more universal feel. However, Escalante's fourth feature is also his strangest and one of the most uncompromising cult films of recent years. The 'alien' element is a creature that resides in a remote cabin in the countryside and appears to feed off sexual desire. On the surface, it may seem like a significant change of gear for Escalante, but in its social concern – exploring his country's patriarchal culture, and shining a light on homophobia and domestic violence – it remains no less controversial than Escalante's earlier films.

ABEL FERRARA (1951)

— NEW YORK AUTEUR

The very definition of a gonzo filmmaker, Abel Ferrara has forged a career exploring lives *in extremis*, from deranged killers, vengeful victims and sexual deviants to corrupt politicians, cops on the edge and ravenous vampires.

Born in The Bronx, Ferrara is a graduate of SUNY Purchase College. His first commercial feature was the pornographic *9 Lives of a Wet Pussy* (1976), in which he also appeared – opposite his then girlfriend – after one of the actors was unable to 'perform'. But it was his grindhouse horror *The Driller Killer* (1979) that was both his breakthrough film and the one that defined his persona as a wayward and uncompromising filmmaker. Ferrara starred as the eponymous killer, a frustrated artist, but what stands out now is the film's use of Catholic imagery, an element that reappeared in the director's subsequent work, most notably in the shocking *Bad Lieutenant* (1992).

Ferrara next chalked up a key title in the rape revenge sub-genre with *Ms.45* (1981), also known as *Angel of Vengeance*. Although mauled by critics on release, the film, like Meir Zarchi's earlier *I Spit on Your Grave* (1978), has been re-evaluated and now stands as a fascinating, if problematic, provocation. It also marked the end of the first phase of the director's career, as the 1980s saw him shift towards the mainstream, directing for television series such as *Crime Story* and *Miami Vice*, as well as the less memorable films *China Girl* (1987) and *Cat Chaser* (1989).

If *King of New York* (1990) hinted at a return to form – and a film that saw Ferrara embark on regular collaborations with a group of acclaimed and daring actors, from Christopher Walken and Harvey Keitel to Matthew Modine and Willem Dafoe – *Bad Lieutenant* marked a career high. In one of his best performances, Keitel plays a corrupt cop living on the edge. A drug and

gambling addict whose manipulation of the law and abuse of his position make him morally irredeemable, Ferrara's character study is a ferocious and unremitting assault on a society teetering on the brink of chaos. With its frequent use of Catholic iconography and even an appearance by Christ before the film's broken anti-hero, *Bad Lieutenant* incurred the wrath of moral groups, outraged by what they saw as an utterly immoral and blasphemous film, not a work that was attempting to come to terms with a society seemingly inured to violence. It quickly became a cult hit, playing the late-night slot in cinemas, and ranks alongside *The Funeral* (1996) and *Welcome to New York* (2014) as one of Ferrara's most admired works. He followed it with the near-incomprehensible *The Blackout* (1997), an off-kilter adaptation of sci-fi noelist William Gibson's *New Rose Hotel* (1998) and cast Juliette Binoche in a film-within-a-film about the life of Mary Magdalene, whose sheer bizarreness ranks alongside his equally eccentric portrait of a tense, psycho-sexual relationship between Keitel's director and Madonna's star in *Dangerous Game* (1993).

However, in terms of cult appeal, none of Ferrera's films since *The Driller Killer* – labelled a 'video nasty' in the United Kingdom and banned by the country's film censors – have matched up to his deranged black-and-white vampire opus *The Addiction* (1995). Melding highbrow discussions around the My Lai Massacre and US guilt over its involvement in Vietnam with orgies of bloodletting, it is, as one critic noted, a 'weird, wild, wired' ride and Ferrara at his most provocative.

66 A SCRIPT IS NOT
A PIECE OF LITERATURE –
IT'S A PROCESS. 99

GEORGES FRANJU (1912-1987)

The importance of Georges Franju's contribution to cinema lies as much in his actions away from the film set as it does in his iconic cult classic and a series of surrealist-inspired wonders.

Born in Fougères, Brittany, Franju served briefly in the French military in Algeria. After being discharged in 1932, he studied to become a set designer and went on to create backdrops for the Folies Bergère. He met Henri Langlois around this time and they codirected the short *The Métro* in 1935; the following year, they set up the Cinématheque Française. Franju left the organisation in the hands of Langlois for four decades before returning to it towards the end of his life, when he was appointed honorary artistic director.

Franju's film career is divided between his early documentaries and later narrative features. His first documentary remains his most shocking. *Blood of the Beasts* (1949) contrasts scenes in an abattoir with life in a Parisian suburb. The juxtaposition of two different worlds became a common element of Franju's work and was used to blistering effect. It is here that the influence of the surrealists can be found. Franju was friends with André Breton and revelled in making strange the ordinary and the everyday, noting: 'It's the bad combination, it's the wrong synthesis, constantly being made by the eye as it looks around, that stops us from seeing everything as strange.'

Franju's most famous film, *Eyes Without a Face* (1960), was released in a watershed year for psychological horror. Michael Powell's *Peeping Tom* and Alfred Hitchcock's *Psycho* also caused a stir among critics and audiences. Franju's film may not have attracted the same level of opprobrium as *Peeping Tom*, but *Eyes* was seen as such a radical departure for the director that it was viewed as a betrayal of his earlier principles. It tells the story of a surgeon who kidnaps and kills beautiful women in order to transplant their faces onto his daughter's, which was badly disfigured in an automobile crash he caused. Its quotient of gore and theatrics saw the film written off for decades, until reappraisal in the 1980s found it acclaimed as a horror masterpiece. Like Franju's subsequent *Judex* (1963), an homage to Louis Feuillade's silent crimes series, *Eyes* is both a cult favourite and a perfect example of Franju's particular view of the world.

66 WHAT PLEASES IS WHAT
IS TERRIBLE, GENTLE
AND POETIC. 99

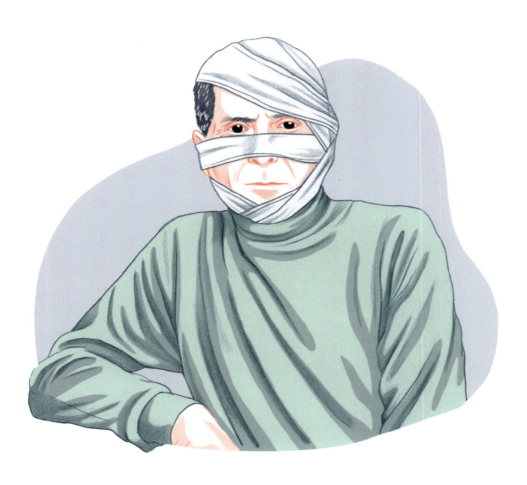

LUCIO FULCI (1927–1996)

—— ITALIAN SHOCKER

Initially known for his comedy scripts, Lucio Fulci gained fame and notoriety as the director of one of the most graphically violent and sadistic horror films ever made.

Born in Rome, Fulci initially trained to be a doctor but then decided on a career as an art critic. Shortly after, he moved into film, initially as a documentary filmmaker and assistant to great Italian directors such as Luchino Visconti, Federico Fellini and Mario Bava. He grafted as a screenwriter for other directors before making his feature directorial debut with *The Thieves* (1959). In contrast to his reputation today, the subsequent decade saw him build his career on a series of commercially successful comedies, particularly the collaboration with knockabout comedy duo Franco Franchi and Ciccio Ingrassia. However, only a handful of films from his first decade as a filmmaker saw international distribution. They reveal Fulci to be a competent, but not inspired, director.

His foray into spaghetti westerns and historical adventures notwithstanding, Fulci's reputation rests on his move into horror, with *Perversion Story* (1969) and *A Lizard in a Woman's Skin* (1971). He initially followed Bava in directing giallo: a brand of Italian horror that blended crime, psychological thriller and the fantastic. But his visual style lacked the flair of his mentor. As he progressed, Fulci's journey into horror saw him cast his net beyond giallo, as evinced by *Zombie Flesh Eaters* (1979). Excessive gore came to the fore, and such scenes as the encounter between a large splinter of wood and an eyeball became the kind of set piece audiences could expect in a Fulci film.

His collaboration with screenwriter Dardano Sacchetti produced a series of films that caused censorship problems in many of the countries they played. If *City of the Living Dead* (1980), *The Beyond* and *The House by the Cemetery* (both 1981) shocked audiences, they only hinted at what was to come. British censors were so shocked by *The New York Ripper* (1982) – a serial killer thriller that Fulci saw as his homage to Alfred Hitchcock – that every print of the film was flown back to Italy. The reputation of this infamous film now defines Fulci's legacy. What sophistication he might have lacked when compared with his giallo peers, he made up for in graphic detail, which few directors have dared or wanted to emulate.

TERRY GILLIAM (1940)

—— MYTH MAKER

Epic is not only the perfect description for many Terry Gilliam's films, but it also represents the ambitions of this visionary director whose off-screen battles are almost as legendary as those he brought to the screen. Most famously, he spent two decades trying to realise his adaptation of Miguel de Cervantes' *Don Quixote*.

Born in Minneapolis, Gilliam moved to London in the late 1960s and worked as a strip cartoonist for *Help!* magazine, where he met John Cleese. That association led to his becoming the 'other member' of the Monty Python team, often playing peripheral characters in sketches but providing the striking animation that linked them. It was a key element in making the show so unique, and the bawdy, youthful humour present in the series has remained a constant throughout much of Gilliam's work.

Fantasy is a recurring element in Gilliam's films, from its playful appearance in his earliest shorts to the layers of myth and the fantastic in *The Man Who Killed Don Quixote* (2018). His first attempt at feature filmmaking – codirecting *Monty Python and the Holy Grail* (1975) with Terry Jones – set the standard that would continue with *Jabberwocky* (1977) and the entrancing *Time Bandits* (1981). These films betray the influence of Gilliam's time with the Pythons: both comprise episodic narratives that play out like a series of interlinked sketches. Low-budget or grandly realised, Gilliam's films evince a preference for lo-fi effects: puppetry and special effects over computer-generated worlds. When he has employed visual effects, the results have been underwhelming. *The Brothers Grimm* (2005), *The Imaginarium of Doctor Parnassus* (2009) and *The Zero Theorum* (2013) disappoint because they lack the elements that make the fabric of Gilliam's worlds so tactile.

Officialdom, or the grey world of bureaucratic doublespeak, is anathema to Gilliam's worldview, but a rich target in his work. It was first witnessed in his short that preceded *The Meaning of Life* (1983). *The Crimson Permanent Assurance* saw an aging business take on corporate giants in a wonderful fantasy featuring skyscrapers as ocean-going battleships. These faceless, pinstriped marauders have been a constant in Gilliam's films and have come to represent the obstacles to him achieving his vision – nowhere more so than in his most fully realised and 'Gilliam-esque' film *Brazil* (1985): an epic, uncompromising, wildly ambitious yet idiosyncratic and deeply personal Orwellian masterpiece.

LUCILE HADŽIHALILOVIĆ (1961)

—— DREAM CATCHER

Associated with the New French Extremity movement, writer-director Lucile Hadžihalilović enigmatically explores youth, gender and sexuality in her alluring, exotic work.

The wonders and pitfalls of growing up lie at the heart of Hadžihalilović's two features and various shorts. The sensitivity and narrative subtlety of her films are a stark contrast to the viscerality of her professional and personal partner Gaspar Noé. Born in Lyon to Bosnian parents, Hadžihalilović studied filmmaking at La Fémis in Paris. Her collaboration with Noé began with her editing his acclaimed short *Carne* (1991) and its feature-length incarnation *Stand Alone* (1998). Between the two, they formed the production company Les Cinémas de la Zone, and she wrote, directed and edited *La Bouche de Jean-Pierre* (1996), a portrait of a young girl living in a problematic domestic situation. It was shot by Noé and screened to critical acclaim at the Cannes Film Festival.

Hadžihalilović's youth was spent on the Moroccan coast, and water plays a significant role in her two features. They are notable for their ethereal atmosphere, creating otherworldly environments that exist in a place between reality and a dream. *Innocence* (2004) unfolds in a girls' school, located deep in a forest. It is a rapturous evocation of youthful abandon, where water elicits both sensuous pleasures and the intimation of danger. The film's colour was manipulated digitally, enhancing the imagery of the scenes shot day-for-night – a process by which night-time scenes are shot in daytime with the film underexposed to give the impression of little to no daylight – and the verdant green of the flora that threatens to consume the school.

A decade passed between Hadžihalilović's first and second features. During that time, she worked on a project that never materialised and helped Noé on *Enter the Void* (2009). Consequently, the arrival of *Evolution* (2015) was eagerly anticipated. A contrast to the closeted world of her debut, it was filmed on the shores of Lanzarote and focuses on young boys and their mothers. The earlier film may edge towards the horror genre, but *Evolution* dabbles in science fiction, albeit of an organic kind that blends exquisite underwater scenes with strange clinical procedures in a near-deserted hospital. Both of Hadžihalilović's features are oblique in their mode of storytelling, and the filmmaker has resisted attempts to offer any explanation. These are films to be experienced and, from there, we can draw our own conclusions.

DENNIS HOPPER (1936-2010)

—— HOLLYWOOD REBEL

Actor, artist, photographer and hell-raiser, Dennis Hopper was as much a part of the Los Angeles art world as he was a Hollywood icon.

Born in Dodge City, Kansas, Hopper moved to San Diego when he was 13, took an interest in acting at school and, by the time he left his teens, had befriended James Dean and starred opposite him in *Rebel Without a Cause* (1955) and *Giant* (1956). As an actor, he excelled at villainous or morally ambiguous characters, such as his role in the John Wayne western *The Sons of Katie Elder* (1965), or later performances in *Blue Velvet* (1986), *Paris Trout* (1991) and *Speed* (1994). In addition to recording life among the film and art set of Los Angeles and New York, Hopper also recorded – and was deeply committed to – the nascent Civil Rights movement. As the 1960s progressed, he became an integral member of the West Coast's countercultural scene, throwing himself into the lifestyle, particularly in terms of his legendary drug consumption, which fed into his era-defining directorial debut with co-writer and co-star Peter Fonda, *Easy Rider* (1969).

The story of two bikers making their way across the Midwest, *Easy Rider* may have held little interest for mainstream Hollywood, but its huge success was noted. The film captured the zeitgeist of America's more rebellious younger generation in the late 1960s, who desperately wanted to break with the conservative past. Hopper not only showed the way, but also highlighted the danger that such behaviour might elicit from those opposed to change. At the same time, the filmmaker's own behaviour was becoming more extreme. He married The Mamas and the Papas singer Michelle Philips in 1970, only to divorce her eight days later, and he began work on his second feature, *The Last Movie* (1971).

Shot in Mexico and detailing a film shoot that goes wildly off the rails, *The Last Movie* is a fine example of life reflecting art. The budget swelled, Hopper disappeared into a drug-fuelled world and the editing process seemed to take forever. It was not the follow-up to *Easy Rider* that the studio had been expecting. However, time has been fairer to the film than critics and audiences were on its release, and it now ranks as one of the great films about filmmaking. Furthermore, the shenanigans that unfolded on set have been immortalised in the documentary *The American Dreamer* (1971), a perfect epitaph for one of US cinema's most iconic mavericks.

KING HU (1932-1997)

—— MARTIAL ARTS MASTER

Few other martial arts directors took the genre to as lofty a height as King Hu, whose best work transformed swordplay into acts of balletic beauty.

Born in Beijing, Hu (his Mandarin name was Hú Jīnquán) showed little interest in cinema when he was young. Instead, he had a passion for the Beijing Opera and comic books adapted from both opera and martial arts tales. In particular, he was fascinated by the legend of the Monkey King, a central character in Wu Cheng'en's *Journey to the West*. Film only began to make an impact on him after his relocation from China to Hong Kong in 1949. There, he worked in the commercials industry as a designer and an English language teacher. It was in this latter role at Great Wall studio, teaching the children of executives, that his proficiency in Mandarin found him working in film. He started out as a set decorator, before becoming an actor in 1954. He moved to the Shaw Brothers Studio in 1958, with an acting contract that included the possibility of a future in directing.

Hu appeared in 37 films over the course of a decade and took on deputy directing responsibilities, to Li Hanxiang, in 1963 with *The Love Eterne*, followed a year later by *The Story of Sue San* (1964). His feature debut was the war film *Sons of the Good Earth* (1965), for which he wrote the screenplay and played the role of a heroic resistance fighter, battling the Japanese. A follow-up was planned, but shelved early in its production due to political sensitivities and a threat of a ban by censors responsible for the Singapore-Malaysia region – a key commercial territory for the Shaws. The cancellation of the project proved fortuitous for Hu, whose next film, *Come Drink with Me* (1966), transformed him into a leading force in the wuxia genre.

" THE AUDIENCE IS THE CAMERA. I DON'T WANT THE AUDIENCE TO SIT AND WATCH, I WANT IT TO MOVE. "

Wuxia, meaning 'martial heroes', is a literary genre that dates back to 300–200 BCE and encompasses stories about roaming heroes whose adventures find them engaging in swordfights. In film, there are examples of wuxia adventures dating back to the 1920s. But Hu's collaboration with Shaw Brothers Studio found the director drawing on his love of Chinese opera, stage choreography and theatricality with resources that allowed him to begin to realise his vision. *Come Drink with Me* established certain elements that Hu embellished in subsequent films, most notably the female protagonist, a skilled swordsperson who earned the respect of her male peers and adversaries. In the film, Cheng Peipei plays the *xia nü* (lady knight errant) Golden Swallow; she was later cast as the villain in Ang Lee's *Crouching Tiger, Hidden Dragon* (2000). Female protagonists also dominate Hu's

subsequent *Dragon Inn* (1967) and *A Touch of Zen* (1971): two masterpieces that remain pinnacles of the genre. Notably, Hu took wirework – employing wires to help actors fly through the air – to new heights, while his use of the traditional Chinese tavern as a microcosm of society has been replicated in countless films since.

Although Hu's style of cinema had become unfashionable by the late 1970s, films such as *Crouching Tiger* and *House of Flying Daggers* (2004), with homages to memorable fight scenes from his films, highlight the enduring popularity of the filmmaker's greatest work.

JIM JARMUSCH (1953)

—— INDIE GODFATHER

If John Cassavetes is the godfather of US independent cinema, then writer, director, musician, part-time actor and raconteur Jim Jarmusch is its perennially cool older sibling.

Born in Cuyahoga Falls, Ohio, Jarmusch claims his early film education came from his mother, a former local film and theatre critic, who would leave him during the day at various screenings in a nearby cinema. His earliest memories there are of 1950s monster movies, such as *Creature from the Black Lagoon* (1954). He saw his first adult film, *Thunder Road* (1958), when he was just seven years old, and it left an indelible impression upon him. The influence of these films, a mix of genres and lowbrow cinema are present in Jarmusch's work, rubbing up against his love of literature and arthouse tendencies to create a unique style of filmmaking whose vernacular – often spoken by intellectual drifters, petty criminals or societal outliers – is a joyful blend of existential rumination and the knowingly smooth syntax of movie cliché.

While studying at Columbia University, with hopes of being a poet, Jarmusch spent a summer working in Paris, passing most of his time at the Cinémathèque Française. On his return to New York, he enrolled on a film course at Tisch School of the Arts and also immersed himself in the punk and no wave culture emerging from the city. His debut feature *Permanent Vacation* (1980) and his international breakthrough *Stranger Than Paradise* (1984) helped define the aesthetics of no wave. However, his subsequent Louisiana crime comedy *Down by Law* (1986) and the episodic narrative strands of the Elvis homage *Mystery Train* (1989) and five-city taxi-centred comedy *Night on Earth* (1991) saw Jarmusch move into his own, idiosyncratic, sublimely funny landscape.

His early low-budget films were noteworthy for their easy-going charm and dialogue, but it was the stark revisionist western *Dead Man* (1995), shot in striking black-and-white, and the samurai-mafia urban comedy thriller *Ghost Dog: The Way of the Samurai* (1999) that furthered Jarmusch's reputation as one of the finest filmmakers of his generation. Although playing with recognisable genres, both films defy categorisation. It is an element that has defined his subsequent work, whether engaging with vampires in *Only Lovers Left Alive* (2013), middle-age crises in *Broken Flowers* (2005) or the day-to-day felicities of human interaction in *Paterson* (2016). In all, Jarmusch's deadpan humour, matter of fact incidents and deep, heartfelt compassion for his characters reinforce his position as a poet filmmaker on the landscape of US cinema.

JEAN-PIERRE JEUNET (1953)

— FRENCH STYLIST

Jean-Pierre Jeunet is known for a dazzling visual style, and his most inventive feature arguably remains his dark, idiosyncratic debut.

Jeunet has had two chapters in his life as a director. Since 1997, he has worked solo on projects. Before that, he was a co-director with the animator and cartoonist Marc Caro on *Delicatessen* (1991) and *The City of Lost Children* (1995). It is because of these films that Jeunet became a cult sensation.

Born in the Loire, France, Jeunet studied animation at Cinémation Studios and met Caro at an animation film festival at Annecy in 1977. Over the next decade, they produced a series of acclaimed shorts and music videos, before embarking on their feature debut, *Delicatessen*. A live-action film that could easily have been a wildly surreal animation, *Delicatessen* presents an extraordinary vision of a post-apocalyptic world. Set in and around an apartment block above a butcher's shop, whose constant supply of meat comes from a grim source, Jeunet and Caro's film is driven less by a strong narrative than by a series of interconnected vignettes. Its influences encompass German expressionism and the more recent Cinéma du look, as well as generations of physical comedians, from Buster Keaton to Jacques Tati. The film

also cemented the collaboration between Jeunet and the actor Dominique Pinon, who appeared in the director's previous short *Things I Like, Things I Don't Like* (1989) and went on to play a role in all of Jeunet's subsequent features.

The chaotic nature of fate lies at the heart of Jeunet's work, whether it is that of two potential lovers in *Amélie* (2001), a woman searching for her husband in the horror of the battlefields of World War I in *A Very Long Engagement* (2004), a man seeking revenge against the arms industry in *Micmacs* (2009) or a young genius setting out into the world alone in *The Young and Prodigious T.S. Spivet* (2013). The singularity of Jeunet's worldview jars against the dictates of a studio, as was highlighted when he took on *Alien: Resurrection* (1997), the fourth film in the popular and successful franchise. A few Jeunet-like touches notwithstanding, it remains his least characteristic work. But these later films, even when traversing the dead-strewn fields of a horrific conflict or detailing the impact of an out-of-control arms industry, feel more than a few shades lighter than *Delicatessen*, with its perfect balance of sweet innocence and jet-black humour.

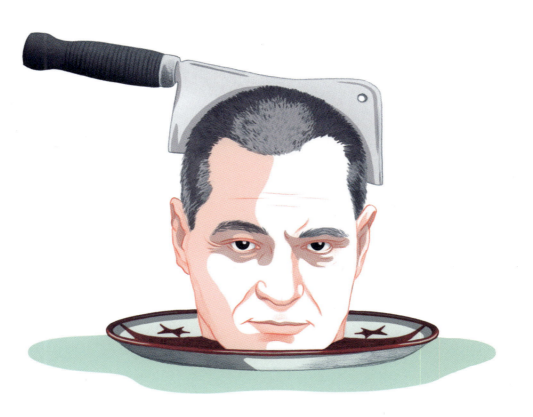

BETWEEN 17 AND 21, I WAS A WORKER IN THE TELEPHONE COMPANY AND IMAGINATION SAVED MY LIFE.

ALEJANDRO JODOROWSKY (1929)

—— MASTER OF THE ABSURD

The spiritual founder of the midnight movie, Alejandro Jodorowsky is a visionary director whose cinema is a drug-addled trip through strange worlds, including his own past.

Jodorowsky's greatest cult film might just be the one he never made. In 2013, the filmmaker, who was born in the north Chilean city of Tocopilla, appeared in Frank Pavich's documentary *Jodorowsky's Dune*, an account of his attempts in the mid-1970s to adapt Frank Herbert's sprawling science-fiction epic. Intended to be a 14-hour opus, the film far exceeded its budget and was never realised. However, the book that Jodorowsky produced with his collaborators has since become the stuff of legend and has been hugely influential over subsequent visionary science-fiction films. In the same year the documentary came out, Jodorowsky released the first of two magical realist–inspired fictional autobiographical films, *The Dance of Reality*.

(It was joined in 2016 by *Endless Poetry*). Like his vision for *Dune*, these films underpin the irreverence, visual ingenuity and surreal imagination of this singular filmmaker.

Jodorowsky has always blended politics, genre filmmaking, the influence of art movements and the carnivalesque into films that are as unclassifiable as they are wildly entertaining. Beyond his role as director, producer, screenwriter and frequent actor in his films, he is a composer, novelist and comics writer, painter, sculptor, mime artist and theatre director. The son of Jewish immigrants from what is now Ukraine, Alejandro Jodorowsky Prullansky experienced an unhappy childhood – he claims he was the result of his father raping his mother in a fit of jealousy – and witnessed first-hand US imperialism through the activities of a mining company in Tocopilla. He immersed himself in reading, became involved in

> **MAYBE I AM A PROPHET. I REALLY HOPE ONE DAY THERE WILL COME CONFUCIUS, MUHAMMAD, BUDDHA AND CHRIST TO SEE ME. AND WE WILL SIT AT A TABLE, TAKING TEA AND EATING SOME BROWNIES.**

theatre and eventually moved to Paris in his early 20s to study mime. He directed his first short there, *Les Têtes Interverties* (1957), followed by his first comic strip, *Anibal 5*. He moved to Mexico in 1960, where he directed his feature debut, an avant-garde adaptation of Fernando Arrabal's play *Fando y Lis* (1968). It caused a minor riot when it premiered at the Acapulco Film Festival and was subsequently banned in Mexico.

El Topo (1970) not only remains Jodorowsky's most famous film, but also it was the feature that started the midnight movie trend. A wildly surreal take on the western, with the filmmaker in the title role, it follows a gunslinger and his son on a journey through a post-apocalyptic desert landscape on a quest for enlightenment. Drawing heavily on Christian symbolism and Eastern philosophy, the film depicts the gunslinger as he takes on four challengers,

each representing a religion or philosophy. With its wild ferocity, the film soon found a following, including an ecstatic John Lennon. Ben Barenholtz, the owner of New York's Elgin Theater, chose to take a chance on the film when no other distributor would show it and screened the film in the late-night slot, where it remained, playing seven days a week for six months.

Jodorowsky's subsequent work, from *The Holy Mountain* (1973) to *Santa Sangre* (1989) to more recent films, continues the style set out in *El Topo*, but the filmmaker never quite achieved the sense of doom-laden wonder that he scored with that strange, quixotic and disturbing masterpiece.

> **MOST DIRECTORS MAKE FILMS WITH THEIR EYES; I MAKE FILMS WITH MY TESTICLES.**

HARMONY KORINE   (1973)

—— CHRONICLER OF AMERICA'S UNDERBELLY

The writer behind one of the most controversial films of the 1990s transformed into an uncompromising filmmaker with an offbeat perspective of the world.

Harmony Korine was born in California but raised in Nashville, Tennessee. His father encouraged an interest in circuses, whose freak-show elements played a significant role in aspects of Korine's work. Other influences included time spent living in a commune, which fed into the environment Korine created for *Mister Lonely* (2007), and a passion for the films of German filmmaker Werner Herzog, who stepped in front of the camera as a bullying father in Korine's family drama *Julien Donkey-Boy* (1999).

After high school, Korine moved to New York. He hung out on the streets, picked up the vernacular and thought his future lay in professional skateboarding. It was while hanging out with friends that he encountered photographer and fellow skateboarder Larry Clark, who commissioned him to write about his experiences. The screenplay that became *Kids* (1995) was delivered three weeks later, and the film – a frank tale of sex and violence among teens – was seen by critics as a wake-up call regarding youth culture in the United States.

Korine's films explore the underbelly of US society. His approach has attracted criticism: that his work is barely coherent and visually cacophonous. Others see a filmmaker breaking down film language and rebuilding it with a radically different grammar. Across five features as director and two as a writer, Korine has engaged with mental illness, life below the poverty line, dysfunctional childhood and the extremes of contemporary college life. Anyone shocked by *Kids* will likely have been aghast at *Gummo* (1997), his directorial debut, and *Julien Donkey-Boy*. They are as unconventional as Korine, whose antics outside of his films have attracted significant attention. Most notoriously, he embarked on the project *Fight Harm* (1999), which saw him provoking strangers to fight with him.

Until recently, Korine has remained an outlier on the landscape of US cinema. Both *Mister Lonely* and *Trash Humpers* (2009) evidenced his unwillingness to compromise. However, *Spring Breakers* (2012) saw him break through to a larger audience. It focuses on four college friends and their experience during spring break in the Florida town of St. Petersburg, where thousands of students party for the holidays. Wildly colourful and amoral in its portrait of the excesses of this hedonistic world, Korine's film is a dayglow fever dream – a John Hughes film on acid.

BARBARA LODEN   (1932–1980)

—— AMERICAN OUTLIER

An actor and director of the stage and screen, Barbara Loden cemented her reputation with an extraordinary standalone feature as director.

Loden was born in Asheville, North Carolina. Following her parents' divorce, she lived with her devoutly religious maternal grandparents in an environment that she referred to as emotionally impoverished. However, the community provided her with more than enough colour and experience to create the richly detailed backdrop for *Wanda* (1970).

Loden moved to New York when she was 16 and began a modelling career, followed by a stint as a pin-up girl and a dancer, before enrolling at the Actors Studio. She married the film producer and distributor Larry Joachim, who helped her get a role on the popular television comedy review *The Ernie Kovacs Show*. Stage roles followed, but her breakthrough came in *Wild River* (1960) and then *Splendour in the Grass* (1961). Both films were directed by Elia Kazan, whom Loden married in 1966 after a long-standing affair. They separated in the late 1970s and planned to divorce, but Loden's terminal cancer diagnosis halted the proceedings.

Kazan directed Loden in 1966 in a stage production of Arthur Miller's *After the Fall*, loosely based on the playwright's marriage to Marilyn Monroe. It earned her the best notices of her acting career and she won a Best Actress Tony award. She returned to the screen in the adaptation of John Cheever's *The Swimmer* (1968), but was famously cut out of the film following a dispute between the film's director and producer. Frustrated, Loden decided to create a project that would suit her talents. She found the perfect source material in the story of Alma Malone, who had been convicted for her part in a bank robbery. The detail that attracted Loden to the story was Malone's thanking the judge for imprisoning her – a relief compared with the life she had experienced up to that point. A friend loaned Loden the money to develop the project and when she couldn't find a director, she chose to make the film herself.

Wanda is groundbreaking not only for being one of the only US films directed by a woman at that time, but also because it challenged the conventions of mainstream US cinema. The film won the Critics Prize at the Venice Film Festival and it also screened at Cannes. Loden died before she could complete another feature; *Wanda* remains her legacy and one of the finest debuts by a US filmmaker.

<blockquote>
" I TRIED NOT TO EXPLAIN
THINGS TOO MUCH IN
THE FILM, NOT TO BE
TOO EXPLICIT, NOT TO
BE TOO VERBAL. "
</blockquote>

DAVID LYNCH (1946)

— SUBVERSIVE SURREALIST

Artist, musician, writer and director David Lynch is surrealism's renaissance man: a gifted filmmaker whose talent has long been too vast for one medium.

Has any other director done more than David Lynch to overturn the Rockwellian image of small-town America? If his terrifying dream fever of a nightmare *Eraserhead* (1977) employed a post-industrial backdrop to flesh out the director's fervid imagination, subsequent features have painted a portrait of modern America, whose glistening aspirational veneer coats a darker world of violence, misanthropy and sexual degeneracy, where innocence is only maintained through ignorance.

Lynch was born in Missoula, Montana, and was childhood friends with Jack Fisk, the acclaimed production designer who worked on many of his films. They both attended the Pennsylvania Academy of the Fine Arts, where Lynch studied art, but also became involved in film, directing his first short *Six Men Getting Sick (Six Times)* (1967). His subsequent short, *The Alphabet* (1968), became a calling card to the American Film Institute (AFI), which awarded him a grant to make *The Grandmother* (1970), whose surreal, dreamlike style presaged his subsequent features.

Eraserhead began to take shape while Lynch was studying at the AFI Conservatory in the early 1970s, but took five years to complete. It was then turned down by most major festivals, even Cannes. A screening at the Los Angeles Film Festival was attended by Ben Barenholtz, the distributor at New York's Elgin Theater, and Lynch's film joined *Night of the Living Dead* (1968), *El Topo* (1970) and *Pink Flamingos* (1972) as one of the key midnight movie cult successes. Critical opinion of the film has since been revised, and it is now regarded as a surreal

masterpiece, with the late Stanley Kubrick once listing it as one of his favourite films.

Lynch dabbled with the mainstream, both successfully with *The Elephant Man* (1980) and far less so with the uneven *Dune* (1984), the latter of which he turned down *Star Wars: Episode VI – Return of the Jedi* (1983) in order to make. *Dune* may be his least personal work, but the films and television series he produced over the course of the subsequent decade defined Lynch as a singular and uncompromising visionary. *Blue Velvet* (1986) opens in the manner of other small-town American dramas produced in the 1980s, but it soon turns those worlds on their head, offering up an initially unsettling, eventually terrifying portrait of a world riddled with corruption and crime. He continued in the same vein, but becoming stranger, in *Wild at Heart* (1990) and *Lost Highway* (1997), along with a segue into television with

the *Twin Peaks* series (1990–1991) and its more terrifying movie spin-off *Fire Walk with Me* (1992). Lynch even channelled his vision towards Hollywood with his noir masterpiece *Mullholland Dr.* (1999).

Although the filmmaker's feature output has slowed in recent years, his work in other areas, from fine art to photography, has continued unabated. A memoir, *Room to Dream* (2018), co-written with Kristine McKenna, offers some insight into his work, but typically raises more questions than it is ever prepared to answer.

GUY MADDIN (1956)

— EARLY CINEMA

Few filmmakers have used their work to cast an eye on cinema's past with such unique vision as Canadian writer-director Guy Maddin.

To watch a Maddin film is to be transported into a strange, ethereal world that is both oddly familiar and yet never existed. Merging modern technologies with the techniques of early cinema, Maddin's films are a visual delight, exploring themes that were considered taboo in the early years of the twentieth century.

A towering physical figure, Maddin grew up in Winnipeg, Canada, which is the fictional backdrop of *My Winnipeg* (2007), a loosely autobiographical portrait of the city and its history, and the third in the director's 'Me Trilogy', after *Cowards Bend the Knee* (2003) and *Brand Upon the Brain!* (2006). Maddin arrived at filmmaking after studying economics at university and taking on a variety of jobs. He became interested in cinema through a friendship with the experimental filmmaker and lecturer Stephen Snyder, who held weekend film screenings at his house. They became Maddin's film education before he enrolled on a film course at Manitoba University under the tutelage of Snyder, whose work – alongside David Lynch's *Eraserhead* (1977) and *Un Chien Andalou* (1929) by

Salvador Dalí and Luis Buñuel – had a lasting influence on him.

Maddin made his feature debut with *Tales from the Gimli Hospital* (1988), much of which was shot in his aunt's hairdressing salon. Along with his subsequent *Archangel* (1990), it was shot on 16mm and in black-and-white. That sophomore feature, set at the end of World War I, played with the part-talkie style that was employed by many films after the emergence of sound in the late 1920s. With the significantly larger budget he received to produce *Careful* (1992), Maddin faced demands to make a colour film. He responded by adopting the two-colour Technicolor style of the early 1930s. It set a template for the kind of films that Maddin would subsequently make, drawing on the tropes and techniques of earlier cinema while their exploration of sexuality and desire to transgress norms remain contemporary.

Maddin is a singular presence on the landscape of contemporary film, and his collaborative efforts, which include *The Forbidden Room* (2015, co-directed with Evan Johnson) and *The Green Fog* (2017, co-directed with Evan and Galen Johnson), have only expanded the scope of his work, being both a celebration of cinema's rich history and extraordinary film works in their own right.

RUSS MEYER (1922-2004)

── FELLINI OF THE SEX INDUSTRY

Few other filmmakers have explored their peccadillos on the screen as thoroughly as Russ Meyer, the 'king of the nudies'.

Best known as a director and producer, Meyer was also a writer, editor, cinematographer, actor and stills photographer. His work, though firmly entrenched in the sexploitation genre, was also recognised for its campy humour and satirical take on the hypocrisy of moral standards in the United States.

A native of California, Russell Albion Meyer began making films when he was 15. He continued making films during World War II, working as a combat cameraman for the Army Signals Corp. Without contacts in the film industry, Meyer failed to gain work as a cinematographer in Hollywood. Instead, he became a movie stills photographer, working on high-profile films such as *Giant* (1956), and as a glamour photographer for publications such as *Playboy*.

Meyer's breakthrough as a director came with his $24,000 budget comedy *The Immoral Mr. Teas* (1959), which went on to gross more than $1 million on the independent US cinema circuit. Like his subsequent work, Meyer distributed his own films, which was time-consuming but resulted in his turning around a significant profit that enabled him to further his ambitions. His early work, though better in quality than most of the nudie films populating the circuit, differed little in structure, with a thin wisp of a narrative linking together scantily clad or fully undressed women. It was in these early films that Meyer's preference for large-breasted women became clear.

Lorna (1964) marked a shift in Meyer's style and was the first of his classic period, when he produced his most striking films. Black-and-white replaced colour, with the resulting saving allowing the filmmaker to take more risks with his narrative. His films were no longer a series of 'sexy' scenes, but offered up a provocative storyline in which women tended to win out over their male counterparts in a battle of the sexes. By *Faster Pussycat! Kill! Kill!* (1965), Meyer had refined this approach to near-delirious levels. An exploitation film about three violent go-go dancers on the rampage along a mostly deserted desert highway and featuring an iconic performance by Tura Satana as Varla, the leader of the gang, the film presages the rise of counterculture in the United States and the shift in gender politics. It remains Meyer's most notorious film.

OSCAR MICHEAUX (1884-1951)

—— BLACK CINEMA PIONEER

One of the most important and pioneering US writers, directors and producers, Oscar Micheaux is nevertheless an absent figure in many histories detailing the development of cinema.

In 1986, Spike Lee released *She's Gotta Have It*, now seen as the vanguard of a generation of films by African American filmmakers. In the same year, the Directors Guild of America awarded Micheaux a Golden Jubilee Special Directorial Award, 35 years after his death. He changed the course of filmmaking for African Americans, at a time when racism remained rife in US society and the rhetoric of the Ku Klux Klan was increasingly vocal because of the huge box-office success of D.W. Griffith's *The Birth of a Nation* (1915). Micheaux challenged the representation of black lives and culture on the screen.

Born to former slaves in Illinois, Micheaux moved to Chicago when he was 17. After feeling cheated at the way employers took advantage of him, he set up his own shoeshine stand. From there, he became a Pullman porter, a relatively well-paid job that allowed him to travel the length and breadth of the country. Having saved enough money, he bought a homestead in South Dakota. As one of the few black farmers in the region, he began to write articles and long-form pieces about his experiences and aspirations. His breakthrough came with the publication of his mostly autobiographical novel *The Conquest: The Story of a Negro Pioneer* (1913). In 1918, Micheaux was offered money for the film rights to the book by Lincoln Motion Picture Company, but realised that he wanted complete control over production and instead set up the Micheaux Film & Book Company. Contacting potential patrons he had met as a Pullman porter, he offered shares in his company that allowed him to proceed with filming. In 1919, he unveiled *The Homesteader* to generally favourable reviews and healthy box-office receipts.

Over the next 30 years, Micheaux produced more than 40 films. His silent films mostly comprised melodramas, with a sharp social or political message: *Within Our Gates* (1920) may not have been a direct riposte to Griffith's earlier racist tract, but its depiction of lynchings and racist behaviour challenged *The Birth of a Nation*'s falsities. The arrival of sound posed technical problems, but Micheaux's ambition shone through. In all, the black experience remained key, and his films never shied away from fractiousness within black communities, as well as the many challenges from outside.

TAKASHI MIIKE (1960)

— JAPANESE GORE MAESTRO

To describe Takashi Miike as prolific barely encompasses the vast output the filmmaker has notched up over the course of two decades.

A Takashi Miike film is a difficult thing to classify. There are certain themes that run through his work, but he employs genre conventions as malleable entities, bending them to his will and creating weird and wild entertainments that might start out as one thing and end up as something completely different. Take *Audition* (1999), arguably the director's widest seen film. It begins with banter between two male friends. One has lost his wife and the other, a film producer, suggests setting up a fake casting audition in the hope of finding him a date. The chosen woman soon takes the upper hand, the film grows darker – although never losing its darkly comic edge – and ends up with a violent climax that involves amputation and a cheese wire. And yet, as shocking as that scene is, it pales compared with the violence in other more notorious Miike films, such as *Ichi the Killer* (2001).

Miike was born in Tokyo and studied film at Yokohama Vocational School of Broadcast and Film, under legendary Japanese filmmaker Shohei Imamura.

He may have learned the syntax of film there, but he was trained to work at speed and with maximum efficiency in the television industry. His professional career began by cranking out television productions to extremely tight deadlines. He also took on direct-to-video projects, which gave him more creative freedom. In his first four years as a filmmaker, he churned out nine films. His productivity has rarely slowed since, so much so that by the time he was celebrated at the Cannes Film Festival in 2017 for his 100th feature, *Blade of the Immortal*, he had already begun work on his 101st, *JoJo's Bizarre Adventure: Diamond Is Unbreakable Chapter I*, one of his many manga adaptations.

Miike made his theatrical debut with *The Third Gangster* (1995), but it was *Shinjuku Triad Society*, completed later that year, that attracted attention. It featured the director's trademark use of extreme violence and characters who existed either in the criminal underworld or had links to it, and whose behaviour often tipped towards the erratic or downright bizarre. Even in Miike's more 'conventional' films, such as the political thriller *Shield of Straw* (2013), he still pushes the limits of the genre with an over-the-top climax.

GASPAR NOÉ (1963)

—— FRENCH EXTREMIST

The French writer-director is one of the architects behind the New French Extremity movement and an arch-provocateur of modern cinema.

Few contemporary directors attract as much rancour and outrage as Gaspar Noé. Sex, violence, death, drugs, bodily excretions and the corporeal nature of our existence are constants in his work, which is also technically dazzling and journeys to corners of the imagination that few filmmakers dare to go.

The son of Argentine abstract artist Luis Felipe Noé, Noé studied cinema and photography at the École Nationale Supérieure Louis Lumière. He has spoken of his love of films from the late 1970s and early 1980s, such as Dario Argento's *Suspiria* (1977), George A. Romero's *Dawn of the Dead* (1978), Andrzej Zulawski's *Possession* (1981) and Gerald Kargl's *Angst* (1983). But he has also highlighted the influence of Stanley Kubrick, whose attention to detail and constant searching for new ways to explore and present cinematic imagery in films like *2001: A Space Odyssey* (1968) are reflected in Noé's technical virtuosity. His preference for long takes is accompanied by vertiginous camerawork, giving his images a weightlessness that finds its audience on the ground one moment and careering over a crowd, building or city the next.

Sex has remained a constant throughout Noé's films, from his shocking breakthrough short *Carne* (1991) to *Climax* (2018), a thrilling dance-driven orgy of drug-fuelled paranoia. He constantly strives to explore the act in its various forms, while nudity is employed less as a provocation than as a natural state. If the exploration of consensual sex is ever-present in Noé's work, his representation of sexual violence is, appropriately, shocking: so much so that the rape scene that dominates Noé's most controversial film, *Irreversible* (2002), is unwatchable. In contrast to his usual fluid camerawork, Noé's extended single shot is static, his camera instead lying motionless on the floor. There is no titillation, just utter repulsion at what is happening.

The extreme nature of Noé's work has placed him at the vanguard of New French Extremity, a movement of filmmakers exploring the transgressive in contemporary society. Nowhere is Noé's interest in the body more explicit than in his tour de force *Enter the Void* (2009). Both a seductive dream and startling nightmare, it opens with the death of its protagonist, who then takes viewers on a gravity-free journey through Tokyo's seedy nightlife. A blur of neon and bodies, it is a sensory experience quite unlike anything else.

GORDON PARKS (1912–2006)

— ## RENAISSANCE MAN

Gordon Parks was one of the 20th century's key photographers, a gifted musician, and, as a filmmaker, one of the pioneers of the Blaxploitation genre.

Parks' spot in the limelight began some three decades before he picked up a movie camera. As a budding photographer in the mid-1930s, his recording of African American life in and around Chicago resulted in Parks being invited to join the photography department of the Farm Security Administration (FSA), working alongside Walker Evans and Dorothea Lange, and charged with documenting poverty and the struggles faced by families in Depression-era rural America. With the rise of the Civil Rights movement in the post-war era, Parks became a key figure in documenting its activities and the oppression it faced. At the same time, he became one of the only black photographers to be commissioned by mainstream style magazines for fashion and celebrity shoots.

In the 1950s, Parks gradually increased his work in the film industry, initially shooting documentaries on African American life. Then, in 1969, he became one of the first major black directors in Hollywood with his adaptation of his semi-autobiographical novel *The Learning Tree* (1963). It ended up being one of the first films to be preserved by the National Archives of the United States, part of a wider library of archive material highlighting Parks' importance to 20th century US cultural history. Like his subsequent films, it found him articulating the challenges facing black communities in the United States, highlighting economic disadvantages and racial prejudice. It was shot in an unfussy, naturalistic style, as were his later *Leadbelly* (1976), a stark portrait of the legendary blues singer, and the acclaimed television film *Solomon Northup's Odyssey* (1984) – later filmed as *12 Years a Slave* (2013) by Steve McQueen.

Parks' hugely influential second feature *Shaft* (1971) was imbued with a style that reflected the times, but never at the expense of naturalism or his gift as a storyteller. It was one of the key early entries in what became known as the Blaxploitation genre: films that, at their best, focus on prioritising – and lionising – black protagonists, often portraying white characters and archetypes negatively, and presenting a critique of the economic racial divide in US cities. John Shaft is presented as an anti-hero with whom black audiences could engage and identify. The film's influence, alongside that of Parks' other extraordinary endeavours, has been long and lasting: director Spike Lee, for example, has cited Parks as a key inspiration to his career.

GEORGE A. ROMERO (1940–2017)

Raising zombies from the dead and helping to bring horror into the modern age, George A. Romero has had a lasting influence on genre filmmaking.

Night of the Living Dead (1968) remains one of the great midnight movies. It tested the limits of what could be shown to mainstream audiences and proved to be a breakthrough for the fledgling filmmaker.

Born in the Bronx, Romero learned the rudiments of filmmaking by renting film reels from a Manhattan company to screen at home. After graduating from Pittsburgh's Carnegie Mellon University, and following a brief stint as a gofer on Alfred Hitchcock's *North by Northwest* (1959), Romero became a commercials director. He set up a production company with a group of struggling but ambitious filmmakers, which produced his first clutch of films, including his landmark horror feature debut.

Although now established as a classic, *Night of the Living Dead* was initially a critical and commercial failure. It was only when the film began to do the rounds on the late-night cinema circuit that it built up a sizable following. Over the course of the next four decades, it spawned five sequels, whose themes offer up a withering critique of US society and values. They encompass anti-Vietnam rhetoric, the nuclear family, consumerism, reactionism in Reagan's America, concerns over the military scientific complex and class division. The last is a central theme in *Land of the Dead* (2005), whose scenes of the undead (read the economically disadvantaged) rising out of a river powerfully evoked media images broadcast in the immediate aftermath of the devastation wreaked by Hurricane Katrina.

The critical and commercial high points of Romero's career were the second and third *Dead* instalments: *Dawn of the Dead* (1978) and *Day of the Dead* (1985). They employed excessive gore, which increasingly became a staple of the horror genre during this period, while offering up a perfect blend of thrills, scares and laughs. In his other films, most of which fall within the horror genre, Romero was no less playful. He revised the vampire genre with *Martin* (1978) and domesticated the monster genre with *Monkey Shines* (1988). His films' influence is both significant and wide-ranging, impacting younger generations of filmmakers and horror writers. The zombie genre would never have existed in the way it does without Romero. As such, the most appropriate homage to his work is Edgar Wright's *Shaun of the Dead* (2004), a smart and affectionate pastiche of a zombie-infested world.

KEN RUSSELL (1927–2011)

— ENGLISH PROVOCATEUR

Few British filmmakers have been as controversial or as outspoken as Ken Russell, a writer-director, memoirist and photographer, whose flamboyant personality was as notorious as his work.

It would take a hardy person to claim to like all of Russell's films without reservation: not because Russell's films over his 40-year career ran the gamut from high art to kitsch exploitation, but because of their wildly varying quality. Occasional accusations of misogyny, blasphemy and homophobia notwithstanding, Russell has, at various times, been heralded as a filmmaker of great talent, a fascinating biographer of classical composers, an artist exploring and exploiting the fringes of popular culture and a cult director whose finest works are compelling and visionary.

Born in Southampton, Russell started his career as a freelance photographer and documentary filmmaker. He was noted for his photo-essay on teddy girls in *Picture Post*, and for his early short films, particularly *Amelia and the Angel* (1958), which attracted the attention of the BBC. Employed to work on the influential arts magazine programme *Monitor*, Russell soon showed an aptitude for directing expressive documentaries that interspersed interviews with dramatic recreations. He was especially drawn to biographical profiles of classical composers.

Although Russell's *Billion Dollar Brain* (1967) proved he could deliver a mainstream studio hit, and *Women in Love* (1969) balanced the controversy of D.H. Lawrence's novel with images of sublime beauty, the filmmaker's subsequent career was dominated by outrage and controversy – both on and off the screen. As his films became more outrageous, he took on the personality of a flamboyant, dandy-like character who never seemed afraid to speak his mind. During this shift, Russell continued to produce portraits of classical composers, but the films increased in their bizarreness. Changing gear musically, Russell's version of The Who's rock opera *Tommy* (1975) revelled in excess. No less controversial, the filmmaker's diptych of sexual perversion in the United States, *Crimes of Passion* (1984) and *Whore* (1991), shocked audiences and critics, with the latter's commercial failure pretty much destroying any chance Russell had of continuing his career in the mainstream.

Despite this, Russell's films feature moments of breathtaking beauty. *The Devils* (1971), arguably the closest he came to a masterpiece, is an extraordinary vision of an apocalyptic world. A provocation above all else, it is what Russell should be remembered for, its depth and passion anathema to the momentary celebrity he achieved towards the end of his career on the television show *Big Brother*.

SUSAN SEIDELMAN   (1952)

—— 8OS PIONEER

The director of an iconic 1980s film that starred one of the era's most recognisable and influential figures, Susan Seidelman brought punk attitude and feminist ideas into the mainstream.

Born in Philadelphia, Seidelman attended New York University Tisch School for the Arts, attracting critical acclaim for her short *And You Act Like One Too* (1976). By the time she graduated, New York had become a cultural hub for the nascent punk and no wave movements. Nan Goldin, Kathy Acker, Kathryn Bigelow and Sara Driver were already making inroads in their various disciplines, encouraging other women to find forms of expression for their stories and views. The cultural scene as a whole became the object of Seidelman's fascination, which resulted in her ultra-low-budget feature debut *Smithereens* (1982). Shot on 16mm and with a roughly hewn aesthetic, it was inspired by Giulietta Masina's character in *Nights of Cabiria* (1957) and was the first independent US film to screen in competition at the Cannes Film Festival.

Few films are as emblematic of a decade as Seidelman's sophomore feature *Desperately Seeking Susan* (1985). It was inspired by French New Wave director Jacques Rivette's *Celine and Julie Go Boating* (1974) and captured Madonna at the height of her newfound fame. Although the singer wasn't the star of the film, her presence contributed significantly to its success. In a story of mistaken identity between Madonna's eponymous rebel and Rosanna Arquette's character, who desperately wants to be like her, Seidelman cleverly tapped into her singer-star's growing appeal. And like *Smithereens*, Seidelman reinvented New York for Roberta, transforming it into the backdrop of a modern-day Alice in Wonderland tale. Madonna's 'Into the Groove' played on the soundtrack, and the film's tapping into the zeitgeist of its pop star and questions of identity pertinent to the 1980s, particularly in terms of gender, found a number of critics naming it one of the best US films of the year and, eventually, the decade.

Making Mr. Right (1987), featuring a goofy performance by John Malkovich, and *She-Devil* (1989), which saw Meryl Streep spar against feature film debutante Roseanne Barr, also found Seidelman imbuing social comedies with a feminist perspective. But neither possessed the edginess or 'of the moment' urgency of *Desperately Seeking Susan*. Seidelman directed the pilot episode of *Sex and the City* and has continued to make films while nurturing future filmmakers at Tisch.

SEIJUN SUZUKI (1923-2017)

— CINEMA'S YAKUZA GODFATHER

Before Quentin Tarantino claimed to make gangsters cool, Japanese writer-director and popular actor Seijun Suzuki wowed audiences with his tales of the Tokyo underworld.

Suzuki's career might have remained in the margins of Japanese cinema had the proliferation in the West of his films on VHS not made him such a cult figure, beloved by Jim Jarmusch and Tarantino, as well as Asian filmmakers such as Wong Kar-wai and Takeshi Kitano, whose own yakuza-themed films evinced a similarly cool, stylised sheen. It was a remarkable turnaround for a director once blacklisted for a decade by his own film industry.

Born in Tokyo, Suzuki was recruited into the Imperial Japanese Army in 1943. He was shipwrecked twice during World War II, both times the result of US attacks on the cargo ships he was aboard. He left the service in 1946 and over the years has reflected

with a darkly comic perspective on his time in the military, even finding humour in the direst of moments. After failing an entrance exam into Tokyo University, Suzuki was informed by a friend that there was a call for entrants to the film department at Kamakura Academy. He progressed from there to a position as assistant director at Shochiku. His recollection of the period was one of mediocrity: 'I was a melancholy drunk, and before long I became known as a relatively worthless assistant director.' Nevertheless, he cut his teeth working with seasoned filmmakers, which allowed him the opportunity to take up a position at Nikkatsu when it reopened its doors after being dormant for nearly 15 years.

At Nikkatsu, Suzuki soon progressed from assistant director to screenwriter with *Duel at Sunset* (1955), followed by his directorial debut *Victory Is Ours* (1956). Between 1956 and 1967 he directed 40

films, an average of more than three a year. His creative breakthrough, in which his style branched out from the studio demands for a steady stream of solid if uninspired B-movies, was *Youth of the Beast* (1963). At this point, Suzuki's films became less bound to narrative conventions and more attuned to wildly stylised visuals and knockabout humour, which set them apart from the work of his peers. This approach culminated in an extraordinary series of yakuza thrillers, comprising *Tokyo Drifter*, *Fighting Elegy* (both 1966) and *Branded to Kill* (1967). The last was made with a reduced budget – punishment for Suzuki indulging in excesses that Nikkatsu executives abhorred. Unfortunately, the result, though beloved by fans and subsequently regarded as a surreal yakuza masterpiece, was the final straw for the head of Nikkatsu, who sacked Suzuki. His legal case against the company saw him blacklisted as a director for ten years, but also led to his iconic status and transformation into an actor.

Suzuki returned to directing in 1977, employed by Shochiku. He directed an acclaimed trilogy – *Zigeunerweisen* (1980), *Kagero-za* (1981) and *Yumeji* (1991) – as well as *Pistol Opera* (2001), a follow-up of sorts to *Branded to Kill*, and finally the ravishing musical love story *Princess Racoon* (2005). Despite this, it is for his great, wildly incoherent, deliriously entertaining 1960s gangster films that he will be remembered.

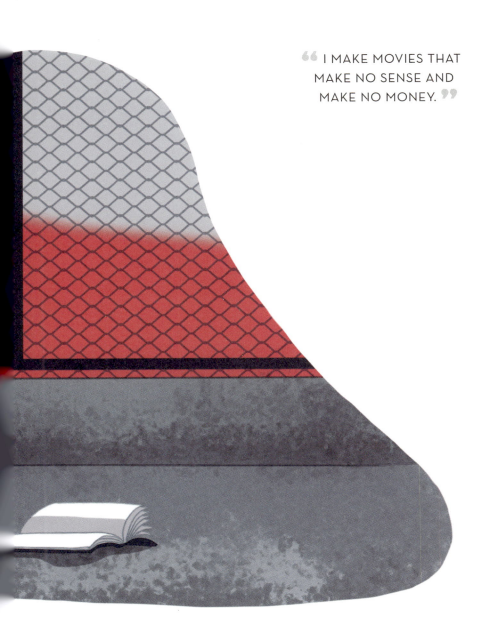

“ I MAKE MOVIES THAT
MAKE NO SENSE AND
MAKE NO MONEY. ”

LARISA SHEPITKO (1938–1979)

—— RUSSIAN VISIONARY

The director made only a handful of films before her untimely death, but Larisa Shepitko's reputation was defined and immortalised by two compelling, stylistically daring works.

The melancholy that pervades Shepitko's small body of work reflects the bitter pain of a life cut short. She was killed in a car crash while scouting locations for her feature adaptation of *Farewell to Matyora* (1976), novelist Valentin Rasputin's account of the impact of industrialisation upon rural life. She was 41 and had completed only four commercial features, two of which are regarded as classics of Russian cinema from this era, but which remain criminally underseen. Her husband, the director Elem Klimov, eventually completed the film, titled *Farewell* (1983), along with *Larisa* (1980), a short tribute to Shepitko.

Born in Artemovsk (Bakhmut as of 2016), Ukraine, Shepitko studied filmmaking at Moscow's All-Union State Institute of Cinematography under the tutelage of the great Soviet montage pioneer Alexander Dovzhenko, until his death in 1956. Her graduation film *Heat* (1963), which presented a fictional account of Russian peasant life, not only won her a college prize and awards at Leningrad's All-Union Film Festival and Karlovy Vary International Film Festival, but also heralded her as a new voice in Soviet cinema. It was during the editing phase of the film that she met her future husband Klimov, and they married in the same year.

Shepitko's interest in the role women play in history is evident in her international breakthrough *Wings* (1966). It tells the story of a former World War II fighter pilot who is now the head of an engineering and construction school. The frustration she feels at the humdrum nature of her existence is borne out in a dream sequence and the film's euphoric and moving end. She followed it with two colour films: the made-for-television musical fantasy *13 PM* (1969) and the relationship drama *You and Me* (1971). However, it was her return to a monochrome world with *The Ascent* (1977), her last completed film, that cemented Shepitko's reputation. Returning to World War II and based on the novel *Sotnikov* (1970) by the Belarusian writer Vasil Bykov, Shepitko presents an existential exploration of two Soviet partisans as they endure a horrendous winter, the brutality of Nazi captors and the questioning of their actions as soldiers. The film's piercing observations only underpin the sense of loss at how much greater a filmmaker Shepitko would have become had she lived.

QUENTIN TARANTINO (1963)

A writer with a gift for the vernacular and a director steeped in cinema's rich history, Quentin Tarantino has built a reputation and impressive body of work out of his love of genre cinema.

If the New Hollywood filmmakers, who include Martin Scorsese, Steven Spielberg and their peers, were the first to reap the rewards of film school, Tarantino represents the video-store generation, whose film education derives from their ability to watch films at cinemas and via VCRs. He was born in Knoxville, Tennessee, but gained entry into the film world when he joined his mother and stepfather in Los Angeles.

Tarantino wrote his first unproduced screenplay, *Captain Peachfuzz and the Anchovy Bandit*, inspired by *Smokey and the Bandit* (1977), when he was 14. He dropped out of high school, lied about his age and became an usher at a porn theatre. Among other odd jobs, he was a store clerk for five years at Video Archives in Manhattan Beach, where he amassed an encyclopedic knowledge of cinema and became known for his recommendations of obscure but essential films. It is this part of his early life that is inextricably bound up with his image as one of the most cinephile of US filmmakers.

What proved to be most refreshing about Tarantino's cinematic worldview was an unwillingness to draw a line between high and low art. A passion for pulp crime fiction informed his interest in highlighting the importance of genre fiction as a key component of US culture. Nowhere is this more evident than in his Oscar-winning feature *Pulp Fiction* (1994). The intersecting stories play out tropes of fictional and cinematic genres, elevated to near-mythical status. The film also highlights Tarantino's delight in casting his favourite actors, whose careers may be seen to be waning, in key roles.

Although *Pulp Fiction* defined Tarantino as one of the hippest US directors of the 1990s, *Reservoir Dogs* (1992) revealed his penchant for extended dialogue scenes, nonlinear storytelling and popular culture. A hit at the Sundance Film Festival, it is regarded as one of the great indie debuts. Since then, the complexity of his work has increased, along with his homages to various influences, from fiction (1997's *Jackie Brown* is an adaptation of Elmore Leonard's *Rum Punch*, 1992) to genre cinema. To watch a film by Quentin Tarantino is to be a student in the filmmaker's idiosyncratic trawl through cinema history.

MELVIN VAN PEEBLES (1932)

— BLAXPLOITATION

Writer, director, musician, singer, playwright and novelist, Melvin Van Peebles is the very definition of the journeyman artist, and also made one of the most searing portraits of racial division in the United States.

Born in Chicago in 1932, after graduating from Ohio Wesleyan University, Van Peebles joined the US Air Force and was based for a time in Germany, where he met his wife, Maria Marx. From there, the couple moved to Mexico, had a son (actor and filmmaker Mario), and Van Peebles took up painting. They then moved to San Francisco, where Van Peebles was employed as a cable car operator. This inspired him to compose a photo-essay based on his experiences, which eventually became his first book, *The Big Heart* (1957). It was while working on cable cars that a passenger suggested he should become a filmmaker.

Hollywood showed little interest in the films of an African American director, but contacts in Europe were more positive and Van Peebles moved to Amsterdam to work for the Dutch National Theatre. It was there that his marriage imploded and his family returned to the United States. He received an invitation from the prestigious Cinématèque Française to show his films in Paris, and while there he began to focus his writing on representing contemporary ghetto life. His development of *Sprechgesang* – a style of delivery

somewhere between speaking and singing – resulted in his debut album *Brer Soul*, which has been a significant influence on hip-hop and rap music. He also adapted his play *La Permission* into his debut film *The Story of a Three-Day Pass* (1968), which finally attracted the attention of Hollywood.

Van Peebles' first feature was *Watermelon Man* (1970), about a white man who wakes up black and thereafter witnesses his life falling apart. But it was his self-funded, singularly independent *Sweet Sweetback's Baadasssss Song* (1971) that defined his career. A provocative exploration of one man's encounters with white authority, it proved to be incendiary politically and made stars out of the then-unknown Earth, Wind & Fire, who performed Van Peebles' score. The film was also responsible for launching the Blaxploitation genre: films about black characters and featuring a predominantly black cast.

Baadasssss!, the making of *Sweet Sweetback*, was directed by Mario Van Peebles in 2003 and highlighted the cultural and political importance of the film and his father's place as one of the most significant African American directors since Oscar Micheaux. Van Peebles senior continues to make films, still produces music and has recently moved into video art.

LARS VON TRIER (1956)

—— ARTHOUSE ENFANT TERRIBLE

Writer, director and perennial enfant terrible, Lars von Trier is arguably the most polarising figure in contemporary European cinema.

In 2011, at the Cannes Film Festival's press conference for *Melancholia*, his mesmerising portrait of one woman's descent into profound depression, von Trier made a series of comments relating to Hitler that attracted universal ire. Even his star, Kirsten Dunst, attempted to stop him mid-flow, realising the likely fallout of his words, no matter how much they were made in jest. It is not the first time that von Trier has caused controversy at such an event, and for many these incidents and comments have become inseparable from his work. After all, his films are works that skirt with fascist symbolism and sadism as much as they are genre-defying dramas that attempt to rewrite the rules of how films should be made.

Lars Trier (the 'von' was added as an homage to the filmmakers Erich von Stroheim and Josef von Sternberg) was born in Copenhagen to parents living in a 'free love' commune. His response to this lifestyle as a teenager was to rebel, preferring the more ordered world of Catholicism. That decision prompted a life-long obsession with the boundaries we build to define our lives. But never content to merely live by the strictures of the church or his own self-imposed catechism, von Trier has pinballed between strict observance of rules and railing against them. This is evidenced in his offbeat documentary *The Five Obstructions* (2003), which saw him reshooting a scene from a film he admires, Jørgen Leth's experimental *The Perfect Human* (1967). Leth informed von Trier of the different ways he was to film each scene and punished him cinematically if he broke the rules.

Likewise, the ten rules of the Dogme 95 movement, which von Trier co-wrote with Thomas Vinterberg and which resulted in his *The Idiots* (1998), attempted to shake up the way directors approach the making of a film. But as these became a new form of practice, von Trier rebelled against them, looking instead for a different way of presenting his dramas. The results were an anti-musical, *Dancer in the Dark* (2000), and two dramas that unfold in near-empty rehearsal spaces, *Dogville* (2003) and *Manderlay* (2005).

Although some audiences refuse to see past von Trier's theatrics and his desire to provoke, others see the presence of genius. In his finest moments, von Trier comes close to achieving the emotional intensity of his cinematic idol and fellow Dane Carl Theodor Dreyer. He can also create breathtaking imagery, from the squalid worlds and film noir scenarios of his early *Europa* trilogy (1984–1991) to the sight of two worlds colliding in the prelude of *Melancholia*. His penchant for shocking audiences continues, as evinced by his longer pornographic version of the already explicit *Nymphomaniac* (2013) and his violent portrait of a serial killer in *The House That Jack Built* (2018). Outrageous, sublimely beautiful, provocative and disturbing, it is impossible to deny or ignore the impact of von Trier's films.

" YOU KNOW, I REALLY DO HAVE SOME MORALS. I DO ACTUALLY CARE ABOUT PEOPLE. AND I DO HAVE A POLITICAL STANDPOINT. "

JOHN WATERS (1946)

—— KING OF KITSCH

There is good and bad taste, and then there's John Waters. The multi-hyphenate artist has transcended his career as a filmmaker to become the brand of his unique perspective on the world.

In his book *Shock Value*, Waters states: 'To understand bad taste one must have very good taste'. The line between the two is one that Waters has crossed throughout his career, so much so that for many people there are two John Waters. Creeping ever closer to mainstream tastes is the director of *Hairspray* (1988), *Cry-Baby* (1990) and *Serial Mom* (1994). Then there is the 'depraved' filmmaker, who made such shocking films as *Multiple Maniacs* (1970) and *Pink Flamingos* (1972). A connoisseur of kitsch with a wicked sense of humour and a penchant for outrage, Waters has established himself as a witty raconteur, outré style guru and artist who transgresses cultural and moral taboos.

Born in the Baltimore suburb of Lutherville, Waters was friends with Glenn Milstead, who as Divine became both his muse and star. Waters' mother claims that *Lili* (1953), which features a strange puppeteer, had a huge impact upon her son, resulting in his presenting violent Punch and Judy shows to his friends and acquiring a taste for behaviour outside societal norms. Waters later claimed that *The Wizard of Oz* (1939) was the most influential film to him in terms of cinema's potential.

As much a fan of Ingmar Bergman and Federico Fellini as he is exploitation directors William Castle and Herschell Gordon Lewis, Waters makes films that draw heavily from high and low culture, as well as from his own life experiences. *Cry-Baby*'s focus on a 1950s 'drapes' gang recalls the filmmaker's own memories of gangs and the murder of a 'drapette' that was reported in a local newspaper. But few audiences could have been prepared for the worlds Waters presents in *Multiple Maniacs*, *Pink Flamingos*, *Female Trouble* (1974), *Desperate Living* (1977) and *Polyester* (1981), for example. These early films were frequently banned and almost always attracted the ire of moral groups.

As the 1980s progressed, Waters toned down the shock value of his work, but his gift for satire and highlighting hypocrisy among the middle class continued unabated. His outrageousness notwithstanding, he has become an institution: in 1985, the presiding mayor of Baltimore proclaimed 7th February John Waters Day. And his persona has shifted, too. Once an iconoclast on the periphery of US film, he is now an icon of US popular culture. His stand-up shows sell out internationally, and his place as a singular filmmaker is assured.

NICOLAS WINDING REFN (1970)

—— KINETIC CONNOISSEUR

As a writer-director with a penchant for extreme violence, Nicolas Winding Refn's journey towards the mainstream has not diminished the intensity of his vision.

Born in Copenhagen into a filmmaking family, Winding Refn claims that in his youth and in rebellion to his parents' passion for the French New Wave, he became fixated with US exploitation films, which informed his work more than any traditional cinematic canon. Initially wanting to be an actor, he studied at New York's prestigious American Academy of Dramatic Arts, but was expelled in the first year. Since then, apart from a few minor cameos, Winding Refn has steadfastly remained behind the camera.

Winding Refn's early Danish language work focused on lowlifes in the Copenhagen underworld. His films exude the kinetic style of Martin Scorsese's early New York features, as he charts his characters' falls from grace. Winding Refn has since learned to temper the urgency of these films with more tranquil moments, which accentuate the brutality of the violence when it comes. Whereas the characters in the *Pusher* trilogy (1996–2005) and *Bleeder* (1999) rush headlong towards their own demise, later films play with pace and draw on a wider array of influences to explore the characters' worlds, from David Lynch for *Fear X* (2003) to Walter Hill for his international breakthrough *Drive* (2011).

There is a perversity to the way Winding Refn deploys his stars. Although Ryan Gosling had the perfect vehicle in *Drive* – his smouldering intensity the perfect fit for the near monosyllabic but ruthless Driver – the actor's role in *Only God Forgives* (2013) takes that archetype and transforms it into a Freudian case study. In his earlier *Bronson* (2008), Winding Refn pushed Tom Hardy to deliver what remains his most outrageous performance, in arguably the strangest prison-set biopic, with its segues into vaudeville.

Music has remained key to Winding Refn's oeuvre, sometimes even defining his films. *Drive*'s cult status is derived in part from composer and former Red Hot Chili Peppers band member Cliff Martinez's 1980s-inspired soundtrack. He also worked with the filmmaker on *Only God Forgives* and *The Neon Demon* (2016), his scores the perfect sonic accompaniment to Winding Refn's neon-soaked worlds. And these worlds, each wildly different, provide audiences with an uneasy balance of bravura camerawork, wild style and bloodletting on an operatic scale. *Drive* may have given him a taste of mainstream success, but Winding Refn seems hell bent at risking everything to ensure audiences never experience the same thing twice in his films.

EDWARD D. WOOD JR. (1924-1978)

—— B-MOVIE ICON

Often dubbed the worst filmmaker in movie history, Edward D. Wood Jr. was a novelist and low-budget genre filmmaker whose films exude a kitsch value that transcends their quality.

Most people know of Wood because of Johnny Depp's portrayal of him in Tim Burton's lovingly made biopic. Shot in black-and-white, *Ed Wood* (1994) captures the wonder of a man with little creative talent who desperately wants to enter the movies. It is a romantic film that looks upon its subject fondly, gently mocking his films but never as cruel as the notices the filmmaker received when *Glen or Glenda* (1953), *Jail Bait* (1954) and the infamous *Plan 9 from Outer Space* (1959) were initially released.

Burton's film ends before Wood's early death, of a heart attack, at the age of 54. He was still living in Hollywood, but by the 1970s he existed in a state of extreme poverty and alcoholism and was heavily dependent on his friends' support. Although his death passed unnoticed, subsequent appraisals of his life, including Rudolph Grey's 1992 biography upon which Burton's film is based, championed Wood's pioneering spirit; his films may have been less than artful, but his resilience in continuing to make them was something to behold.

Wood was born in Poughkeepsie, New York, and from an early age was obsessed with cinema. He collected memorabilia of the stars that cinemas would discard after a film's run and became an usher at a local cinema. His passion was westerns, along with the horror and monster movies that were popular at the time. With the United States' entry into World War II, he was drafted into the army and fought in the Battle of Tarawa, where he lost his front teeth and was shot in the leg.

In 1947, Wood moved to Hollywood and began life as a screenwriter. He wrote

> **ONE IS ALWAYS CONSIDERED MAD WHEN ONE PERFECTS SOMETHING THAT OTHERS CANNOT GRASP.**

a poorly reviewed play of his experiences in the war and wrote, produced, directed and starred in his feature debut *Glen or Glenda*. Semi-documentary in form, the film's admittedly crass portrayal of a cross-dresser, loosely based on transwoman Christine Jorgensen, was informed by Wood's own experience. His mother, Lillian, had wanted a daughter and dressed him in girl's clothes when he was young. As a result, cross-dressing was natural to Wood, and the film was uncharacteristically empathetic to its LGBT theme. The voiceover that narrates the action was supplied by Bela Lugosi, the original screen Dracula, whom Wood had long admired. They became friends and Lugosi appeared in a number of the director's key productions. Most notably, he was the alien vampire in *Plan 9 from Outer Space*. The recipient of the accolade 'Worst Film Ever' at the Golden Turkey Awards, Wood's ineptly made

sci-fi romp remains his best-known film. Although his subsequent work showed little improvement, Wood's name and some of his films live on through an array of references in popular culture, from song titles and lyrics to remakes of his films and scripts, and even a musical, *Dreamer* (2017), about his life.

BRIAN YUZNA   (1949)

— MASTER OF SPLATTER

Although he is better known as a producer, Brian Yuzna's cult status rests on an audacious, jaw-droppingly gory directorial debut, whose reputation has only grown with time.

With the advent of home video in the 1970s, it became possible to make a small fortune from feature filmmaking if you could produce a movie on a low budget and appeal to a wide audience. Nowhere was the recipe more successful than the straight-to-video horror market. Yuzna was one of the key US horror producers to emerge through this route, and whose films featured production values of high enough quality to warrant the occasional cinema release.

Brian Yuzna was born in the Philippines, and it was during a peripatetic childhood, growing up in Nicaragua, Puerto Rico, Panama and the United States, that he first began experimenting with a Super8 camera. He claimed his initial training came through watching François Truffaut's *Day for Night* (1973), which mostly takes place on a film set. An encounter with a film crew on location in Cartagena inspired Yuzna to purchase a 16mm Bolex and to attempt his first film, but it was not until *Society* (1989) that he directed his first commercial feature.

After making the unreleased *Self Portrait in Brains*, about an artist who blows his brains out onto a canvas, Yuzna moved to Los Angeles and met the director Stuart Gordon. Their first collaboration, *Re-Animator* (1985), an adaptation of an H. P. Lovecraft tale, featured such an outrageous amount of gore that it got the pair noticed, and the film went on to become a key horror of the 1980s. Another Lovecraft adaptation, *From Beyond* (1986), followed and cemented Yuzna's status as a horror producer with a keen commercial sensibility. Most of his films existed in a deranged universe detached from reality, whereas *Society* offered up a wildly surreal portrait of the world Yuzna observed in 1980s Hollywood.

Yuzna's pop trash masterpiece has the rich elite of Beverly Hills literally feeding off the less entitled denizens residing in the City of Angels. Unlike his other productions, which overflow with excess throughout, Yuzna holds off his moment of gore until the extraordinary climax, inspired by Salvador Dalí's *The Great Masturbator* (1929), and played out against the strains of the benign 'Eton Boating Song'. It is a savage political satire that ranks alongside John Carpenter's *They Live* (1988) as one of the great cult genre films of the 1980s.

KEY WORKS

Ana Lily Amirpour
A Girl Walks Home Alone at Night (2014)
The Bad Batch (2016)

Kenneth Anger
Fireworks (1947)
Rabbit's Moon (1950–1979)
Scorpio Rising (1963)
Lucifer Rising (1970–1981)

Gregg Araki
The Living End (1992)
*Totally F***cked Up* (1993)
The Doom Generation (1995)
Mysterious Skin (2004)
Kaboom (2010)
White Bird in a Blizzard (2014)

Darren Aronofsky
Pi (1998)
Requiem for a Dream (2000)
The Fountain (2006)
The Wrestler (2008)
Black Swan (2010)
Noah (2014)
Mother! (2017)

Mario Bava
Black Sunday (1960)
Evil Eye (1963)
Blood and Black Lace (1964)
Planet of the Vampires (1965)
Kill, Baby... Kill! (1966)

Danger: Diabolik (1968)
A Bay of Blood (1971)

Kathryn Bigelow
Near Dark (1987)
Blue Steel (1990)
Point Break (1991)
Strange Days (1995)
The Hurt Locker (2009)
Detroit (2017)

Anna Biller
The Hypnotist (2001)
A Visit from the Incubus (2001)
Viva (2007)
The Love Witch (2016)

Lizzie Borden
Regrouping (1976)
Born in Flames (1983)
Working Girls (1986)

Tim Burton
Pee-wee's Big Adventure (1985)
Beetlejuice (1988)
Batman (1989)
Edward Scissorhands (1990)
Batman Returns (1992)
Ed Wood (1994)
Mars Attacks! (1996)
Sweeney Todd: The Demon Barber of Fleet Street (2007)

John Carpenter

Dark Star (1974)

Assault on Precinct 13 (1976)

Halloween (1978)

The Fog (1980)

Escape from New York (1981)

The Thing (1982)

Big Trouble in Little China (1986)

Prince of Darkness (1987)

They Live (1988)

In the Mouth of Madness (1994)

Park Chan-wook

Joint Security Area (2000)

Sympathy for Mr Vengeance (2002)

Oldboy (2003)

Lady Vengeance (2005)

I'm a Cyborg, But That's OK (2006)

Thirst (2009)

The Handmaiden (2016)

Benjamin Christensen

Häxan (1922)

Michael (1924, actor only)

The Devil's Circus (1926)

Věra Chytilová

Daisies (1966)

Fruit of Paradise (1970)

The Apple Game (1977)

Trap, Trap, Little Hat (1998)

Sofia Coppola

The Virgin Suicides (1999)

Lost in Translation (2003)

Somewhere (2010)

The Bling Ring (2013)

Roger Corman

Machine-Gun Kelly (1958)

House of Usher (1960)

The Little Shop of Horrors (1960)

Dementia 13 (1963, producer)

The Raven (1963)

The Trip (1967)

Bloody Mama (1970)

Boxcar Bertha (1972, producer)

Caged Heat (1974, producer)

Roger Corman's Frankenstein Unbound (1990)

Alex Cox

Repo Man (1984)

Sid & Nancy (1986)

Straight to Hell (1987)

Walker (1987)

Highway Patrolman (1991)

Death and the Compass (1992)

David Cronenberg

Shivers (1975)

The Brood (1979)

Videodrome (1983)

The Fly (1986)

Dead Ringers (1988)

Naked Lunch (1991)

Crash (1996)

A History of Violence (2005)

Claire Denis

Chocolat (1988)

No Fear, No Die (1990)

Beau Travail (2000)

Trouble Every Day (2001)

35 Shots of Rum (2008)

White Material (2009)

High Life (2018)

Amat Escalante

Sangre (2005)

Los Bastardos (2008)

Heli (2013)

The Untamed (2016)

Abel Ferrara

The Driller Killer (1979)

Ms. 45 (1981)

King of New York (1990)

Bad Lieutenant (1992)

The Addiction (1995)

The Funeral (1996)

Welcome to New York (2014)

Georges Franju

Blood of the Beasts (1949)

Passing by the Lorraine (1950)

Hôtel des Invalides (1952)

Eyes Without a Face (1960)

Thérèse Desqueyroux (1962)

Judex (1963)

Lucio Fulci

A Lizard in a Woman's Skin (1971)

Zombie Flesh Eaters (1979)

The House by the Cemetery (1981)

The Beyond (1981)

The New York Ripper (1982)

Terry Gilliam

Jabberwocky (1977)

The Time Bandits (1981)

Brazil (1985)

The Adventures of Baron Munchausen (1988)

The Fisher King (1991)

12 Monkeys (1995)

Lucile Hadžihalilović

La Bouche de Jean-Pierre (1996)

Innocence (2004)

Nectar (2014)

Evolution (2015)

Dennis Hopper

Easy Rider (1969)

The Last Movie (1971)

Out of the Blue (1980)

Colors (1988)

The Hot Spot (1990)

King Hu

Come Drink with Me (1966)

Dragon Inn (1967)

A Touch of Zen (1971)

Legend of the Mountain (1979)

Jim Jarmusch

Stranger Than Paradise (1984)

Down by Law (1986)

Mystery Train (1989)

Dead Man (1995)

Ghost Dog: The Way of the Samurai (1999)

Broken Flowers (2005)

Only Lovers Left Alive (2013)

Paterson (2016)

Jean-Pierre Jeunet

Delicatessen (1991)

The City of the Lost Children (1995)

Amélie (2001)

A Very Long Engagement (2004)

Micmacs (2009)

Alejandro Jodorowsky

El Topo (1970)

The Holy Mountain (1973)

Santa Sangre (1989)

The Dance of Reality (2013)

Endless Poetry (2016)

Harmony Korine

Kids (1995, writer)

Gummo (1997)

Julien Donkey-Boy (1999)

Mister Lonely (2007)

Trash Humpers (2009)

Spring Breakers (2012)

Barbara Loden

Wild River (1960)

Splendour in the Grass (1961)

Wanda (1970)

David Lynch

Eraserhead (1977)

The Elephant Man (1980)

Blue Velvet (1986)

Wild at Heart (1990)

Fire Walk with Me (1992)

Lost Highway (1997)

Mullholland Dr. (1999)

Guy Maddin

Tales from the Gimli Hospital (1988)

Careful (1992)

Twilight of the Ice Nymphs (1997)

Dracula: Pages from a Virgin's Diary (2002)

The Saddest Music in the World (2003)

My Winnipeg (2007)

The Forbidden Room (2015)

The Green Fog (2017)

Russ Meyer

Lorna (1964)

Faster Pussycat! Kill! Kill! (1965)

Vixen! (1968)

Beyond the Valley of the Dolls (1970)

Up! (1976)

Supervixens (1975)

Oscar Micheaux

The Homesteader (1919)

Within Our Gates (1920)

The Devil's Disciple (1926)

The Exile (1931)

Takashi Miike

Rainy Dog (1997)

Audition (1999)

Dead or Alive (1999)

Ichi the Killer (2001)

The Happiness of the Katakuris (2001)

13 Assassins (2010)

Gaspar Noé

Carne (1991, short)
I Stand Alone (1998)
Irreversible (2002)
Enter the Void (2009)
Love (2015)
Climax (2018)

Gordon Parks

The Learning Tree (1969)
Shaft (1971)
Shaft's Big Score! (1972)
Leadbelly (1976)

George A. Romero

Night of the Living Dead (1968)
The Crazies (1973)
Dawn of the Dead (1978)
Martin (1978)
Day of the Dead (1985)
Monkey Shines (1988)
Land of the Dead (2005)

Ken Russell

Women in Love (1969)
The Devils (1971)
Lisztomania (1975)
Tommy (1975)
Altered States (1980)
Crimes of Passion (1984)
The Lair of the White Worm (1988)

Susan Seidelman

Desperately Seeking Susan (1985)
Making Mr. Right (1987)
She-Devil (1989)

Seijun Suzuki

Fighting Elegy (1966)
Tokyo Drifter (1966)
Branded to Kill (1967)
Pistol Opera (2001)
Princess Raccoon (2005)

Larisa Shepitko

Wings (1966)
The Ascent (1977)

Quentin Tarantino

Reservoir Dogs (1992)
True Romance (1993, writer)
Pulp Fiction (1994)
Jackie Brown (1997)
Django Unchained (2012)
The Hateful Eight (2015)

Melvin Van Peebles

Watermelon Man (1970)
Sweet Sweetback's Baadasssss Song (1971)

Lars von Trier

Europa (1991)
The Kingdom (1994–1997)
Breaking the Waves (1996)
The Idiots (1998)
Dancer in the Dark (2000)
Antichrist (2009)
Melancholia (2011)

John Waters

Multiple Maniacs (1970)
Pink Flamingos (1972)
Polyester (1981)
Hairspray (1988)

Cry-Baby (1990)
Serial Mom (1994)

Nicolas Winding Refn

Pusher (1996)
Fear X (2003)
Blood on My Hands: Pusher II (2004)
Bronson (2008)
Drive (2011)
Only God Forgives (2013)
The Neon Demon (2016)

Edward D. Wood Jr.

Glen or Glenda (1953)
Jail Bait (1954)
Bride of the Monster (1955)
Plan 9 from Outer Space (1959)

Brian Yuzna

Re-Animator (1985, producer)
From Beyond (1986, producer)
Society (1989)

INDEX

Ian Haydn Smith is the editor of Curzon Magazine and the author of *The Short Story of Photography*. Other publications include a monograph on Wim Wenders, *New British Cinema: From Submarine to 12 Years a Slave* (with Jason Wood) and the forthcoming *The Short Story of Film*. Formerly the editor of the International Film Guide, he is the update editor of *1001 Movies You Must See Before You Die*.

Kristelle Rodeia is a freelance illustrator based in Paris. After studying Plastic Arts and Graphic Design, she is now a full time illustrator working in a mixture of pen, ink and digital drawings. Previous clients include *Stylist*, Veneta Bottega and *Erratum*.

First published in 2019 by White Lion Publishing,
an imprint of The Quarto Group.
The Old Brewery, 6 Blundell Street,
London, N7 9BH,
United Kingdom
T (0)20 7700 6700
www.QuartoKnows.com

Every effort has been made to trace the copyright holders of material quoted in this book. If application is made in writing to the publisher, any omissions will be included in future editions.

A catalogue record for this book is available from the British Library.

ISBN 978 0 71124 026 1
Ebook ISBN 978 0 71124 027 8

10 9 8 7 6 5 4 3 2 1

Design by Paileen Currie
Illustrations by Kristelle Rodeia

Printed in China

MIX
Paper from responsible sources
FSC® C016973